T0128205

THE UNCOMMON COMMON SENSE OF CONQUERING YOURSELF

The Invisible Hands

JAMES H. MENDOZA

authorHOUSE®

AuthorHouse™
1663 Liberty Drive
Bloomington, IN 47403
www.authorhouse.com
Phone: 1 (800) 839-8640

Scripture taken from the King James Version of the Bible.

Published by AuthorHouse   02/10/2017

ISBN: 978-1-5246-5809-0 (sc)
ISBN: 978-1-5246-5807-6 (hc)
ISBN: 978-1-5246-5808-3 (e)

Library of Congress Control Number: 2017900273

Print information available on the last page.

This book is printed on acid-free paper.

INDEX

DISCLAIMER

I declare that my ideas expressed in this book are solely my personal opinions. I based them on my personal observations of my conscious experiences over the last 55 years of my life; I also based them in some concepts and opinions of other authors and inclusions of some readings from the Bible. The tools I used were my instincts, meditation and my common sense, uncommon in me. So I am just an insignificant observer of life, licensed and bestowed by God through inspiration, making me a simple messenger, carrying a message to those who decide to receive it. The right by which I emit my personal opinions to society is instated on the first amendment to the Constitution of the United States of America.

In God I trust.

PREFACE

I hope that these compendium of ideas will provide some of the readers with enough information to keep stimulating some hidden areas of their minds so they can continue formulating questions about life and their surroundings, with the purpose of improving our lives. I would like to make clear that I do not claim to be a saint of any kind; I simply observe life in general with the purpose of finding something useful for all people. I am not dignified at all to get any messages from God or any supreme-conscious mind in any direct sensorial way like sound or sight; the common knowledge waves have come in scarcity to me by inspiration. I have no doubt that the majority of people have had some similar ideas or have experienced the same ideas that I present in this declaration, but they did not have the time or the opportunity to write them as I did. So, may my writings be a reflection of their own ideas, and for that simple reason, feel confident to consider them yours.

Visit us at www.2177club.com or write to me directly to selfconquer@2177club.com for any kind of inquiry or comment.

INTRODUCTION

Most people blindly blame society, our country and the world in general—they are partially right—responsible for many problems in our lives, without really knowing why the real reasons these problems occur. Sociologists, psychologists and investigators of other related professions have analyzed the actions of hundreds of common killers and serial killers during the last fifty years in the USA and have given us information about how these individuals bring misery to people but without a satisfying answer to us about why they do it; what is the real motive of their actions and what kind of solutions we can find to stop these problems for good.

No one can segregate which segment of society these people predominantly come from, because statistics show they come from all strata, giving us the conclusion that all individuals who commit crimes have similar characteristics being the most common denominator a negative emotion called *hate*. I would conclude that this is the main origin of most of our problems, but I think the origin resides in a deeper layer. The experts have described that killers start their malevolent experience at home, then they displace them at their church, synagogue, temple or any place for this purpose used by any other religion or cult, then to school, extending their actions until they end up hurting unknown people, affecting dozens of families and all the society in general. What they have not included is what happens in the mind of those who do not execute these physical crimes, those who control their rage: the general public. In many situations the only difference between these groups is the execution part, because the same brain activity occurs in both groups. I also may conclude that in most cases, people lack one of the most essential elements necessary to keep a healthy society: *love*. This area is the first objective of my empirical observation when I look at the family, the nucleus of society, and its consequences when love-hate affects its life.

We have asked ourselves many questions such as: What is the origin of their rage? Why do these individuals get their motivations from? Why do these people seem to enjoy hurting others? Why cannot they stop their behavior? Why do people get sick? Why do people suffer? Why do people die of heart attacks or strokes? Why do people need to consume products they do not need? Why do people have vices? Why do people have obsessions, compulsions, addictions? In the end, we are without any reasonable answers, but I hope that together, we would be able, at least, to get closer to the threshold of some of these furtive answers to these common questions.

I am using the first step of the scientific method which is the observation and also I use investigations and studies made by different authors in these areas besides the reading of some passages taken from the Bible. To start our investigation maybe if we use our self-introspect and self-retrospect as the initial scaffold of our intangible safari.

To proceed to our observation incursion, I invite you to imagine that you and I are individuals from out of this world who are hovering above the atmosphere for a moment, observing the contours of the planet earth globally, then descending slowly until we observe things that occur down on earth, with all its sounds, images, reasons, motives, personalities, smells, feelings, passions, pains, consequences. Afterwards you will find yourself and then you will identify your own passions, fears, attributes, compulsions, desires, infatuations, injuries, cries, rages, corruptions and more that happen in our own self. But now, if we start observing the steps of how to infiltrate into a dominant country of your choice—once you observe something bigger than you, you would observe yourself with less effort—with the objective to conquer it, we would stablish a starting point. This action would spark a domino effect on the rest of the world so the domination should be fast, controllable and predictable.

The initial step to conquer the dominant country is by putting it under a systematic demoralization through world defamation by all countries alleging accusations of false invasions with the purpose of expansionism by using its influence to introduce its products, industries and ideas into the world communities. At the same time, its domestic rogue groups create turmoil in its societies originating divisions between its population like racial, gender, economical class, etc. These groups set the mental attitude of the general population creating guilt, fear and submission in it, like in the [1]**Stockholm syndrome**.

The second step is by physical world humiliation taking hostages, detonating bombs over big constructions or massive transportation sites and embassies, etc. not only of the targeted country but also of its allies; testing armament like bombs, missiles, rockets in visible scenarios to show off their rebellion to world treaties. The domestic rogue groups use these opportunities to destroy private property and attack members of peace forces.

---

[1] **Stockholm syndrome**, or **capture-bonding**, is a psychological phenomenon described in 1973 in which hostages express empathy and sympathy and have positive feelings toward their captors, sometimes to the point of defending and identifying with the captors. These feelings are generally considered irrational in light of the danger or risk endured by the victims, who essentially mistake a lack of abuse from their captors for an act of kindness. The FBI's Hostage Barricade Database System shows that roughly eight percent of victims show evidence of Stockholm syndrome.

The third step is the personnel infiltration into its government using the law of the land of equal opportunity employment to accept any person from contrary groups or countries, giving them key positions to facilitate any future changes of the law. Here is when the purchasing of newspapers, radio and TV stations by foreigner firms occur. Also the nomination of people with non-credentials are ignored, falsified or just created to fill positions of directors in key agencies occur, etc.

The fourth step is the mental infiltration to control the mind of the people such as the imposition of ideas contrary to its own culture. Also by changing or ignoring the history of the country. Here is when the word discrimination has more weight in its meaning; the lies, the scandals about prominent individuals; the defamation of the country main religion; the world war threats; the distractions through music, sports, pornography, the public-figure scandals and the movie-stars eccentricities, etc.

The fifth step is the physical occupation; slow, invisible invasion through legal or illegal immigration admitting people from countries with opposite ideals. Here is when the hyphenated derivatives of the national country emerge; the ludicrous law suits; the attempts against the first and second amendment of the Constitution; the desecration against the patriot symbols.

The sixth step is the blunt imposition of foreign cultures, languages and religions based on big masses of people with different ideals protesting and demanding their religious and human rights. Here is when the subcultures emerge; when all the news channels and media transmit the same mixed-local-and-foreign news, using the same terminology, acting as if they themselves were foreign to their own country; here is when people destroy the language of the land on purpose by incrementing the use of slangs. Here the culture of the land shows its weakness by adopting foreign rituals accepted as superior. Here is when the simple rules of land like the traffic signs and general public protocols are violated; when human and animal rights become equal, etc.

The capitulation happens when the disruption is obvious, the country has already been divided into heterogeneous groups and the changes are already in place. The selected population gets the green light through government incentives to procreate as if they were termites. Here is when the awaken population becomes aware of the consequences of its moral erosion, but still ignorant that it is the product of a systematic orchestration by some enormous invisible mysterious forces—not defined yet, however, but perceived by many for many generations. Here is when foreigners are elected in main governmental positions because they choose their self-interests over the occupied country but not without the help of bad electors who vote for them for the simple acceptance of some bribes like the affirmative action, food stamps, pro-abortion laws, free cell phones, free housing, political correctness, free driver license, amnesty to illegal immigrants, low sentencing for crimes, parole, free gender-change operations etc.—As if a prostitute had been employed by a licentious businessman just because he wanted to contribute to the economic growth of his domiciliary town.

Lawyers from all stratification levels need to get involved in this process for without them, it would be impossible to handle any of these procedures. Here is when high-rank executives of any company commit white-color crimes without consequences (²**The Enron Scandal**) politicians commit fraud with impunity

---

² **Enron Corporation** was an American energy, commodities, and Services Company based in Houston, Texas. It was founded in 1985 as the result of a merger between Houston Natural Gas and InterNorth, both relatively small regional companies in the U.S. Before its bankruptcy

(³**The Solyndra Scandal**); individuals commit blunt murders on the streets without denunciations from the media on them, only if they belong to some races of their choice. Obviously money, not necessary ideologies only, is a determinant factor in this step,—money is the main stepping stone to the real objective of the contaminated soul, which is power—but if these individuals loved their country, at least they would think about the pain they inflict to the affected families in addition to the consequences of their own moral detriment for exchanging their personal integrity and the safety of their own country for any amount of money.

All these movements are occurring in the world as if some *invisible hands* amassed all the changes at their please. It is difficult to identify *the invisible hands*, but they are governed by those hidden tyrants who control the entire world; some people think they are the long time suspected secret societies well-known to many people for centuries, or simply a world-group of new super-rich people working together just for the final price that absolute-power recipients enjoy—it is unnecessary for me to mention these groups because they are well-known by enough people already, also I do not want to forget any one of them. Alongside it is difficult to find in ourselves the need to analyze the actions of such groups; even though, many

---

on December 2, 2001, Enron employed approximately 20,000 staff and was one of the world's major electricity, natural gas, communications and pulp and paper companies, with claimed revenues of nearly $111billion during 2000. *Fortune* named Enron "America's Most Innovative Company" for six consecutive years. At the end of 2001, it was revealed that its reported financial condition was sustained by institutionalized, systematic, and creatively planned accounting fraud, known since as the Enron scandal.

³ **Solyndra** received a $540 million U.S. Energy Department loan guarantee, the first recipient of a loan guarantee under President Barack Obama's economic stimulus program, the American Recovery and Reinvestment Act of 2009.

have frequently felt their presence in their own socio-economic circles, but to summarize their actions I need to unveil their puppets, portraying them in the form of the four knights of the modern Apocalypse. These knights are tools used by *the invisible hands* before mentioned, although these puppets think and feel they are acting on their own and for their own individual purposes. They remind me the Frankenstein's sub-human experiments that received orders until it came against him, in the end.

The rolls of the four knights are played by:

1- Atheism. This form of religion without an apparent religion is based on hatred towards Jesus because atheists feel individually the center of the universe, one god in each person who believes in the existence of anything—in nothing really—and who deserves everything, so they tacitly proclaim to be the center of society.

2- Communism. This ideology and a form of an economic system is based on the hatred towards humanity. It empowers the few over the masses by declaring the government as the master of the land, raw materials, factories, any instrument of production and the population itself.

3- Islamism. This theocracy implants children with hate towards Christians and Jewish since its self-proclamation as religion about 625 AD. It also dictates its hypnotized followers (the extremists) to conquer the world at any cost (including their own lives), terrorizing their enemies in the name of their god. It constantly pursues to erase history since they plagiarized the Bible of the Jewish and Christians, displacing Christ to a second range of prophets by lying about his life, his resurrection and the conception of his second death.

4- Liberalism. This political viewpoint that in the recent past claims to have some supposed objectives such as the amelioration of political and economic inequalities of society, now it is based on the indiscriminating inclusion of any groups on earth with the mainly objective of gaining votes to perpetrate its power, its demagogy. This originates hate towards innocence in general so the groups they defend do not get exposed to the rest of the population, starting with the simple children's common sense.

These main currents have some things in common: *hate* and the thirst for world hegemony. These strong negative feelings are guided against Judaism and Christianity which have the filters to unveil their real motives. These under-current groups will combine their forces imbibed with motives full of hatred to plot their ways of destruction towards their common enemy, but orchestrated by *the invisible hands*. They are now fighting together against the world, but in the end they will fight against each other and only one will prevail, the one with the highest level of *hatred* within themselves.

Now that we have landed in this country of our experiment we see the confusion of combination of powers creating a domestic problem, carrying our way of self-destruction through the contamination of the ideals which have extended to capitalism. This supposed to be the economic system where the individual, not the government, owes raw materials, factories and any instruments of production that now has become the main tool that *the invisible hands* possess to implement the power they eternally have sought. These actions are visible with the infliction of globalism and monopoly that polarize societies, enriching the powerful with more power to control the minds of the people by keeping them occupied and entertained, looking for their own survival through the confinement of extreme work or by being fanatic followers of sports, pornography, or by the compulsive consumption of material things, keeping them away from their own reality.

Some of the roles of the government is to protect us from foreign enemies like foreign armies or globalism and from domestic enemies like monopolies, but when the government itself mutates to a domestic enemy, then, it cannot defend us at all.

We need to defend our families from these enemies, but we need to change our strategies. We cannot defend ourselves with physical weapons, because the enemy is an invisible legion using its *invisible hands*. The operators control the world as if it were a scenario of puppeteer players with their puppets entertaining their spectators with their intriguing plot in the theatre of life. We need to go back to our basics; we need to understand ourselves; we need to create weapons proper for the job, but first, we need to understand our own mind-operating motives to then profile our enemy by identifying its own operating motives and tools, in this way we will enable us to prepare for this purpose (now we are zooming out from the micro universe to the macro world). We need to go back in time before we were hypnotized into followers. We need to return to our origins to discover how our creator planned our lives for us, and only then we would find the ways to the real human with capabilities of higher potentials without boundaries, to start our personal journey into the infinite space of constant happiness.

The previous description is the scenario of our real world seeing it as if we were watching the beginning of an action movie which usually starts with the problem in the scene of an accident or a crime. The storyteller usually goes back to the beginnings or to previous moments to explain the motives conducing the listener to the present moment, the real time. Similarly, we need to go back to the book of Genesis to see how we were empowered by God after our creation, then to see the moment of our change and then to examine our present life. In other words at the moment that Adam and Eve were thrown out of the paradise. They were changed from spiritual and innocent beings to materialistic individuals until the present humans, but our souls naturally look back for its origin, that is why *the serpent* has to constantly renovate its hypnotic ways on us to keep us within its domains. Such luring occurs by entertaining its subjects through sports, pornography, junk-music, junk-food, alcohol, drugs, compulsive consumption of material things, constant bombarding of new deceptions, etc. During this observation, we will know the reasons why we are also compelled to do things we do not want to do, consequently, we would know the reasons why, they (who are also humans) are compelled to do those manipulations on us. We will understand them and we will not react to their post-hypnotic spells. The next step is to know our predecessor; the moment to begin the identification of your own self.

CHAPTER ONE

THE UNCOMMON-IDEAL HUMAN

Many of us have asked ourselves many questions such as: who am I? What is the reason of my existence? Who created me? Why do I enjoy doing the wrong things? What is the origin of my motivations? Why do I get sick? Why do I suffer of depression, anxiety? Why do I buy products I do not need? Why do I have obsessions, compulsions and addictions? How do entire populations have common ideas? How do some people allow others to control them? How entire populations are dominated? Why do we elect bad dignitaries? Where would I go after I die? These are some of the thousands of questions that people have; for some of them we have answers and some are still in the lab in search for them.

After years of observation, we have realized that we possess some attributes in the form of intuition which, in many occasions, we use to answer some of our questions. Of course my next question is—you probably guest it—what is intuition?

Intuition is the instant knowledge humans detect through an unconscious reception of some information existing in the thin air as if they were radio frequencies received by a radio receptor, emitted by a radio station. As humans have invented the radio (by [4]**Nicola Tesla,** attributed to [5]**Marconi** for years) with an antenna to listen to its programs or in similar manner to use of a modem (modulate-demodulate) to receive a bandwidth to operate the internet, we were created with a natural antenna or with a natural modem (depending of our consciousness level) called the pineal gland to perceive the energy emitted by God, the only problem is that most of us do not know about it and think that our gut-feelings, clairvoyants, premonitions, déjà vu (from French, literally *already seen,* is the phenomenon of having the strong sensation that an event or experience currently being experienced, has already been experienced in the past, like a feeling of recollection), telepathic messages and more, are coincidences of life or are people's tricks, so we treat them as if they are unreal or as if they are not important because those senses are not validated by any authority. As if before any authority's intervention, we were not affected by a simple, invisible force over any object or person on earth called gravity. Did you need [6]**Isaac Newton** to tell you that it exists for you to gravitate?

---

[4] **Nikola Tesla** (July 10, 1856 – January 7, 1943) was a Serbian American inventor, electrical engineer, mechanical engineer, physicist, and futurist best known for his contributions to the design of the modern alternating current (AC) electricity supply system; the remote control, the electrical motor, the wireless telegraphy, the wireless energy supply system, ignored until the present times. The most valuable inventor of all times, but ignored for his menace to the economic powers of his time.

[5] **Guglielmo Marconi** (25 April 1874 – 20 July 1937) was an Italian inventor and electrical engineer known for his pioneering work on long-distance radio transmission and for his development of Marconi's law and a radio telegraph system. He is often credited as the inventor of radio, and he shared the 1909 Nobel Prize in Physics with Karl Ferdinand Braun "in recognition of their contributions to the development of wireless telegraphy".

[6] **Isaac Newton** (December 25, 1642 – March 20, 1726/27) was an English physicist and mathematician (described in his own day as a "natural philosopher") who is widely recognized as one of the most influential

Before we start our journey, let us observe the key to open our mind to other dimensions in life and the reasons why some individuals, who knew about this, hid its knowledge to the masses for their own benefit.

The uncommon-ideal humans are the man and the woman who are simple people who possess the attributes of being telepathic, intuitive, clairvoyant, free, fast learners, inventive,

---

scientists of all time and a key figure in the scientific revolution. His book *Philosophiæ Naturalis Principia Mathematica* ("Mathematical Principles of Natural Philosophy"), first published in 1687, laid the foundations for classical mechanics. Newton made seminal contributions to optics, and he shares credit with Gottfried Wilhelm Leibniz for the development of calculus.

thinkers, respectful, happy, peaceful, energetic, faithful, mentally balanced, honorable, humble, relaxed, patient, scrupulous, moral, confident, fair, determined, disciplined, organized, clean, healthy, positive, dignified, to mention only few. These people start an ideal family which started somewhere in the history of mankind where we cannot find proof of its existence at the precise moment in time historically speaking, but we rely on the Bible to adjudicate that time symbolically to the first couple on earth, Adam and Eve. The historical resources about this matter most of the time are found in cave drawings and some archeological objects of past civilizations; we find proof that man and women were dealing with each other in every day events. In some occasions those findings are in the form of scrolls, written by ancient people. We infer that the way these men obtained knowledge was in the form of inspirations. Who told these people what to say? How to think? How to make conclusions? In essence they describe a family as a man, a woman and children as part of their ancestral basic group. These were normal people forming normal families.

The concept of the word *normal* did not have to be defined in the past, because people applied their common sense to understand it. The word *normal* defines persons, things and behaviors. A person who has a head, torso and limbs, two hands, two legs, etc., is normal and obviously those who have one leg, one arm are not normal because they have a physical impediment. In other words, nature is the artisan of creating normal things, unless, humans intervene in this process affecting the final output. Sometimes chemical leaks combine its structure with natural elements, producing animals, plants and even humans with obvious mistakes. Here we see a two-head snake, a group of people with high incidence of cancer, acephalous children, and things in those areas. Normalcy also includes behavior, not just physical normalcy; so a man moving his body backwards on his hands as a form of displacement would be a case of abnormal behavior. The normal behavior of an uncommon ideal man is a normal conduct with respect to other people's behavior and vice-versa. The word *right*, is the conduct of a subject for doing normal things in favor of the life or preservation of another thing, object or person. The word *wrong*, is the opposite of the word *right*, with respect to the normal person.

Now, the uncommon-ideal man is he who loves to do the right thing in harmony with the normalcy of nature and who wants to keep it that way for the preservation and the betterment of humanity by following nature. The uncommon-ideal woman is the one who follows her uncommon-ideal man to form an uncommon-ideal family with the purpose to produce uncommon-ideal children. But the common practice of the present time is the formation of incomplete families, offering the child the incomplete love from one parent only. The love of only one parent is not enough for children to have balanced souls, because they need the candor, softness and understanding of a mother and the corrective candor and strength of a father. Children only find real love and feel loved in a balanced home, when they are corrected and guided towards the love of God, otherwise they would feel abandoned, reason why they would look for their version of love everywhere else, which is always the wrong source of love. They end up looking for love in another human, in gangs and in vices, always ending in deception and unhappiness. Then it is necessary to form an uncommon-real family in the arrangement ordained by our creator. This arrangement is the one formed by a man and a woman who keep together their normal family with normal children, otherwise, any other combination produces dysfunctional families originating unimaginable problems to society as a result.

The uncommon-ideal woman would not follow another man who were not ideal, but if she formed a couple with him, then, she would become the head of the family by default.

The ideal people's soul are filled with the good spirit, they in turn are happy and have the potential to become like Christ (created in the image of God as written in Genesis 1:27). Happiness is the mind state where a human being is complete and in tune with nature, not needing more than the necessary things to remain alive. Guess who would be unhappy with this idea of people's happiness? The people whose existence depends on the needs of others, they may be the bad politicians, some unscrupulous producers of goods, drug dealers, cult leaders, religions of hate, some minority leaders, pornographers, prostitutes (prostitution is the act of sexually exposing or using the naked or partially naked human body obtaining economical remuneration from it), sports industries, bad lawyers, bad pharmaceutical companies, bad doctors, unions, secret groups (using *the invisible hands* perpetuating their power over the world), etc.

The ideal people are those who love righteousness and live towards its purpose. For religious people it is easier to define it: Those who first love God over anything else.

The ideal people are mentally balanced: happy, honorable, humble, generous, moral, confident, free, discipline, organized, etc. Also they are physiologically balanced or physically healthy. The ideal humans learn from inspiration and feel guidance by their body sensors. They get in communication with other dimensions by navigating the infinite using their soul as their mobile. Their capabilities are endless, but we are not going to concentrate in them in this compendium.

The ideal people do not have compulsions, obsessions or addictions and they are healthy, loving, energetic, peaceful, positive, and confident; disciplined, generous, moral, forgiving, and dignified, just to express some of many more attributes. These people make families—the nucleus of a society. The family starts somewhere in the history of mankind but we cannot find proof of its existence at any precise moment in time. In essence they described a family as a man, a woman and children as part of their basic group—to make progressive countries plethoric of motives to create products and ideas to help others, making their country's progress to a better life for all humanity in general. In the ideal family, grandparents are well integrated into their group forming part of a strong structure because they have experience and wisdom to guide others when necessary, giving society its continuity. They also help to structure society, starting their role with their grandchildren. When children see old people, their minds see respect towards others, forming the bonding core from old to new generation forming a unified and coherent country.

The ideal man is the head of the family with responsibilities to guide his group towards God and to sustain it economically. He is respectful to his wife and children, so his leadership is not by force, but by love. Adam was the one who got the instructions directly from God (Genesis 2:15-18) before Eve was created (Genesis 2:22-23). The ideal woman is subject to her husband when he follows the precepts of God, only to be the head of the family to replace him temporarily when his dignity shrinks by not following God. So she admires her man's leadership and respects his dignity before she loves him. The same way he admires and respects a dignified woman before feeling love for her. This is when they reside in Eden.

Eden represents our life filled with happiness in general, designated to serve its residents by presenting them an entire kingdom which is earth with its plants, minerals, waters and animals for their enjoyment.

THE MISSING LINK

Something happened to humans somewhere on the line of life where we changed our nature and it happened as if it were on purpose. Now, the common people are the opposite of what we have underlined before. Now we are compulsive, reactive, and fearful. We are now angry, revengeful, hateful, insecure, unhappy, dishonorable, prideful, ungenerous, immoral, coward, slave, undisciplined, disorganized, etc. Also we are physiologically unbalanced meaning that we have a tendency to be physically sick.

The organized secret groups, using their *invisible hands*, keep the masses in this unnatural, temporary state through the school system where they have the opportunity to inculcate anything they want into the minds of the emerging new generations. They implant curricula with the intention to indoctrinate children about their mind limitations or anything else they desired to keep the next generation in line with all the impediments necessary to retain them under control. In that way, to produce an intense feeling of unhappiness to perpetrate their final objective which is their complete world power. They know that our natural state is opposite to this new form, which is why they utilize infinite methods of deviation designed to keep us entertained. Why do they do it? If we could listen to the compelling forces in ourselves, we would have already answered this question. Just to remind you that we are made of the same invisible elemental forces that these controlling groups are. I think that this is the real missing link, the mental materialization of limits to our real evolution. There is something missing between the uncommon-ideal human and the common human. The evidence is in the existing of paradigms in our mind. A paradigm is the starting point of anything that involves information in the human thinking defined as a concept, a program of the mind that is designed to keep people thinking in one particular direction outlining a limitation. It is a string of data that contains a command that provides a particular answer to follow a particular line of conduct. An example of a paradigm is written in the book of Genesis that constitutes the first paradigm known to the western world, at least. This happened when God told the first couple, Adam and Eve, that they could eat from all the trees in the garden of Eden, except from *the tree of life* and *the tree of the knowledge of good and evil*; otherwise, they would die, so they believed him, of course, the limitations of the area were well-defined to them. That was an idea planted in their minds and they accepted it as true, because it was true—the trees represent a condition of conduct. God gives almost all his gifts of life but we need to furnish something in return: our conviction to love him. *The tree of life* is the gift to humans when we reach the path to perfection (sainthood). *The tree of the knowledge of good and evil* is when we reach the path to consciousness, given that, once we live, we are solely responsible for our actions, so we are not innocent anymore; therefore, innocence dies. It was until *the serpent* tempted Eve with the doubt that they would not die if they ate the fruit of that tree, and the holy paradigm was broken. This is a paradigm from God over humanity, the problem is that some humans now feel like gods creating their own paradigms and offer them to the rest of humans, playing the role of God.

The most popular human to human paradigm was the theory that earth was the center of the universe, initiated by [7]**Claudius Ptolemy** (100 to 170 AD), an Egyptian astronomer

---

[7] **Claudius Ptolemy** (*Claudius Ptolemaeus*; c. AD 100 – c. 170) was a Greco-Egyptian writer, known as a mathematician, astronomer, geographer, astrologer, and poet of a single epigram in the Greek Anthology. He lived in the city of Alexandria in the Roman province of Egypt, wrote in Koine Greek, and held Roman citizenship. Beyond that, few reliable details of his life are known. His birthplace has been given as

of Greek descend. This paradigm was contradicted by the Polish [8]**Nicolaus Copernicus** (1473 to 1543) theorizing that the earth gravitated around the sun. Thomas Kuhn in his book *The Structure of Scientific Revolutions* mentioned a key term *paradigm shi*ft in reference to the moment of change in these examples. So, if any regime desired to control the mind of a population, it just needed to somehow create paradigms of obstruction in the minds of the people governed and it was for the controlled man to use a paradigm shift to liberate his mind from this yoke. The case of elephant trainers in India is based on this principle when they fret one of the calf legs to a pole for years until the elephant is adult where it is only necessary to tight one of its legs without tighten it to a pole for the elephant to fall under complete control. They do not need to secure the elephant leg to a pole, just because in the mind of the elephant, there is a chain from the pole holding its leg. The same situation has happened to humans for millennia, we think that we are limited to our physical realm; that we need not to worry about the after-life because it is in this world that we can have a good time, so we have to enjoy the present moment conducing ourselves into a dissipated, irresponsible life. In the meantime, the controlling groups who know the truth, feed the consumer's minds to make sure they spend their

---

Ptolemais Hermiou in the Thebaid in an uncorroborated statement by the 14th-century astronomer Theodore Meliteniotes. This is a very late attestation, however, and there is no other reason to suppose that he ever lived anywhere else than Alexandria, where he died around AD 168.

[8] **Nicolaus Copernicus** (19 February 1473 – 24 May 1543) was a Renaissance mathematician and astronomer who formulated a model of the universe that placed the Sun rather than the Earth at the center of the universe. The publication of this model in his book *De revolutionibus orbium coelestium* (*On the Revolutions of the Celestial Spheres*) just before his death in 1543 is considered[by whom?] a major event in the history of science, triggering the Copernican Revolution and making an important contribution to the Scientific Revolution.

money today on things that are, in many cases, unnecessary, but happy and entertained to maintain those reins of power strong. But some people know they are being used, the only thing is that in many cases they have found the wrong ways to oppose the regimes forming groups of opposition using physical aggression as their main course of political pressure. For once they react with violence, they lose their dignified position given that at that point, they change their standpoint, jumping to an area of vulnerability. Those groups have given reasons why the system needs to get rid of them, since they are dangerous to society. They only intuit that real paradigm-change is not by causing fear to others, fulling themselves with impatience, ignorance, discontent and frustration, displacing their rage in a demonstration of tantrums against society. They know deeply in their *unconscious mind* that the changes must be made in our own minds, when we breake the paradigms, the chains that hold our legs fretted to a pole making us to feel like slaves. The mental missing link happened when we believed the lie, losing our faith in God, and shifting our direction to the material world.

THE PINEAL GLAND

We will use this information for the meditation tool later in chapter two. First, locate the crossing point formed by the two perpendicular imaginary lines, the horizontal line starting between your eyebrows and continuing towards the back of the head; and the vertical line starting at the top of your head plummeting towards the bottom of your neck. This point is where the pineal gland is located. In most dictionaries, *the pineal gland* is not defined extendedly, limiting its functions to the secretion of substances called serotonin (this substance causes body alertness) and melatonin (this substance causes body relaxation), but the main functions of this organ are still unknown according to The Taber's Cyclopedic Medical Dictionary; however, the ancient people knew about it as it reads in the Egyptian pyramids and other archeological findings of its periphery. Further studies demonstrated that *the pineal gland* is the door that conducts to other areas of life unknown to us, and when we put this gland to our use, we would extend our consciousness of life, changing our awareness towards our own origins. This type of knowledge is why some secret societies of the world—I find it unnecessary to mention these groups since I am fearful to leave one out, but you will discover them, if you have not done it yet—to have performed certain routines to keep the masses underdeveloped, since if people knew their capabilities, their actions would be more difficult to manipulate (diminishing the powers of any manipulator), that is why when we read: "Humans are created in the image of God. "Let us make man in our image; after our likeness" (Genesis 1:26), some powerful individuals discredited this ideas, mocking them and labeling them as mere mythology. We lost our mental abilities in the past and we have forgotten how the real human supposed to be. The immediate image that comes to mind is the moment in which *the serpent* lied to Eve, convincing her about eating the *fruit* from the tree of *the knowledge of good and evil*. The secret societies know about this idea and want to keep it hidden to all of us, even if it is read by many Bible readers, this information is ignored or simply overseen by many of them. Once you know the path to perfection, your actions would be logical and your interests would be beneficial to humanity. We would not compete with others for trivial things like having a better car, house, image, self-importance, fame, etc. because our kingdom would not be of this world, so any consumed product would be according to our necessities, not to our egocentric mind, we would be thinking about how to help others on improving health, transportation, human developments and living conditions in general, not consuming unnecessary products, cars, airplanes, clothes, houses, pornography, junk-movies, alcohol, junk-food, junk-music, collectives, shoes, etc. in the way we do it, because we would have more control over ourselves. These are few of the thousand effects we are experiencing after we lost the path to our original abilities, but let us focus in finding our way back to them sooner than later.

The pineal gland is referred in the Bible as "the lamp of your body" (Saint Mathew 6:22) and it is the modem by which we receive the messages send by other souls, present in this world or away in other dimensions. The information is similar to any alfa, radio, TV, micro waves or in ways that we even do not even suspect. But certain is that we receive them in our receptive moments through our natural antenna or modem.

All routines in the history of humans have their beginning before they become elemental definitions, in Mathematics, Physics and Chemistry, for example, we use axioms (a formal statement assumed to be true without proof) and in any regular matter we need to define our terminology, similarly, religion uses dogmas in order to develop from that point on to expand into any related application. That is why we needed to define the ideal human first to know our direction, perspective and proportion of our life in society, because, in general, we are part of a group of people who want to live in harmony with each other.

THE HUMAN STRUCTURE

The human being is formed by three different elements that are connected to each other by an infinitesimal electro-magnetic force starting with the soul, the mind and the physical body. They interrelate and form the human as one in a similar way of the Catholic deity, The Father, The Son and The Holy Spirit forming one God within three different entities. The body is the physical dimension and the temple where the mind and the soul are hidden. The mind identifies the person inside it. The soul is the hidden determinant that can push the mind for good or for bad.

ANIMAL AND HUMAN

Animals have instincts, they are amoral, aware of their immediate necessities but unconscious of their existence; they also possess memory to remember places and circumstances that will help them later to find food, water and refuge. They remember places and recognize their herd members, their natural predators and enemies, proceeding according to the circumstance. The limbic system (a very primitive segment of the brain as expressed in the book "Psychosomatics" by [9]**Howard and Martha Lewis**) is the most active area of the brain in animals.

Humans have the same basic elements of animals plus the capacity of loving and hating unlike animals, which turns us moral or immoral, also we are conscious of our necessities and conscious of our existence as [10]**Descartes** declared "I think; therefore, I am", and we also have inspirations which come from our natural core of commands. This is the knowledge that we

---

[9] **Howard R. Lewis** in 1970, he was a government consultant of medical education and a formal editor of Medical Journals. He wrote the books Growths Games and With Every Breath You Take. With his wife, Martha E. Lewis, as co-author, they wrote the books, Psychosomatics, The Medical Offenders.

[10] **René Descartes (Renatus Cartesius**; adjectival form: "Cartesian"; 31 March 1596 – 11 February 1650) was a French philosopher, mathematician, and scientist. Dubbed the father of modern western philosophy, much of subsequent Western philosophy is a response to his writings, which are studied closely to this day. He spent about 20 years of his life in the Dutch Republic.

find in any single human being: The knowledge of good and bad. But the common information that any organism possesses, animal and human, and from which life bases itself is survival, this obviously is contained in the core of our basic information at the moment of conception, when we are a gamete. This means that a fetus is instinctively charged with the compelling effort to defend himself or herself by feeling despair and anguish when in his or her mother's mind crosses an even feeble idea of abortion; the poor, helpless organism feels betrayed. If this fetus becomes an adult, his or her mind will carry these feelings from the *unconscious mind* to the *subconscious mind* to the *conscious mind* at unexpected moments, creating compelling feelings to do things, good or bad, from unrecognized sources for him or her. In the world of plants, if we abandon a land, it would be covered by plants in days and unrecognized after years. The same way with bacteria, if we do not keep clean, bacteria, microbes and fungi they reproduce uncontrollably. So all living creatures: plants, microbe, animals and humans want to live, they want to survive because it is written in their core of instincts, naturally.

HATE

Hate is a negative feeling of the mind that is gestated in our soul, making a person unhappy, envious, malicious, and revengeful. Hate does impose itself, insists on its own way; it does rejoice at wrong and it rejects the right. Hatred is like a worm that gets under our skin looking for residence in our inner self. Hate is a demon that, after finding residence in our mind, becomes very sophisticated enticing us by turning itself undetectable, creating concealments so it could penetrate our soul and invade us with the negative essence of *evil* that most of us have fed for many years, but before us, humanity itself did it for millennia when unconscionably our parents, in retrograde, taught us the way to do it, because they were already invaded by this energy. That is why hatred becomes more sophisticated and uses different masks such as rancor, which in turn becomes even more subtle taking the forms of frustration, resentment, disillusion, deception, depression, doubts, sadness, negativity, fear, wonders, worries, etc., becoming more difficult for us to deal with it after it turns into a major problem because we do not accept that we have been possessed by something different (opposite) to God, and we create excuses, pretexts, justifications why we frequently hold this position against our creator. We take refuge in the form of indulgences and soon we find our immediate force of control: power.

When we experience any of these negative feelings, we are deceived and think we have all the right to be mad, so we want to get revenge and punish the perpetrator, whoever or whatever they represent. We react this way, many times in our mind, and we also do this in the physical-present instant. At this moment, we have a dilemma of possible consequences given that if we react violently towards the subject like a criminal, we might get punished by society, but if we just punish the subject in the comfort of our mind, then we think safely because we are not exposed to external judgment; however, this action derives energy within our physical body guiding us to distractions, indulgences, and later to physical illnesses called *psychosomatic illnesses*. And when we have accepted this condition, we have to justify it and through this, we obtain temporary satisfaction, subsequently temporary pleasure, and then the compulsion to obtain it again, which becomes the food of our evil nature that we already mentioned before. And as we need food to nurture our physical bodies daily, so we need to nurture our soul daily. Once we have a negative soul, our negative feeling called hatred is used to produce negative energy from other sources for consumption by our negative soul, to remain alive, so it needs to find a new source of food daily to satisfy itself. That is why we need to feed our evil nature by hurting others through criticism, condemnation or any form of destruction. Frequently, in similar manner we need to hurt our bodies in the form of tattoos which is a physical mutilation or alteration of the normal body form—a preparation for the satanic mark in our body. In some religions and cults, these physical self-punishment are practiced in the way of kneeling for long periods of time or by self-applying slashes with the intention of compensating their fault with physical pain, soothing the punishment from the deity of his own. Some other form of auto punishment is done by the consumption of any substance to alter our own mind like alcohol or drugs. The evil soul feeds from corruption and sin to grow and to evolve to a new form of darkness, a mutation of evil. Some people call these intangible forms: emotional vampires, emotional leeches, emotional living-dead, demons of a 3rd, 2nd and 1st kinds, etc. The effect that hate provokes in ourselves reflects in different other dimensions of our own being, creating a cascaded-damaging effect to the corresponding levels of human existence. This starts with the soul, then it drips its influence to the mind and it is embraced by the body. Hate is the force, the bonding energy that makes all these feelings attract the form of a unity of unhappiness to each of the human elements.

Some religions are based on this negative energy, making their followers hate everybody who does not belong to it and loving—in their own minds—everybody who belongs to it. This kind of religions are based on Satan's principles because they enjoy destroying, killing, insulting, molesting, hating, stressing, deceiving, degrading, terrorizing, arguing, frustrating, judging, lying, disappointing, demoralizing, resenting, upsetting, traumatizing, depressing and doing anything that will make other individuals unhappy. The members of these kind of religions are only happy, momentarily, when they bring misery to others because at that moment they are feeding the demon they have in their soul. They would never be satisfied, because this stage is for the people who have legions of demons dwelling in their soul. They are ambassadors of hell who only receive instructions and orders from Satan itself. The effect in ourselves when we hate others occurs at different strata creating a cascaded-damaging effect to the corresponding levels of human elements of existence, which are the soul, the mind and the body.

IMPRESSION

Once the mind has been impressed, then the next time the same brain-spot is stimulated, it needs to be altered with at least a soft increment of change in the same direction, this is proved by the effect of alcohol, drugs, cigarettes, defamation, gossip, soap operas, etc. All are addictive in this form besides the chemical elements with addicting properties of their own that affect the physical body as the case of cigarettes (to mention something well-known) that contain hundreds of chemicals in them to affect the user in the form or addictions. This is when the serial killer, to mention a negative extreme for reasons of explaining our case, hurts his next victim with more intensity. No matter if his previous was wild enough, the next experience has to be increasingly more intense. Remember that our soul, under these conditions, needs to be impressed with a higher emotion because this is like our first drink; we are looking for the first original buzz every time we drink, but we do not realize that we need more of the substance the next time we try to encounter that good feeling again.

The forehead impression of *the beast* is not a real number but a real idea imprinted in our mind using the Memes we all know about.

When our soul is imprinted, it is ready to be occupied by any suggestion which later, when we are demoralized, it is converted into a post-hypnotic command. If you would think about the words *sex* and *free*, you would agree. Now let us think about an image, *naked woman*. Now let us add sound, *primitive music*. Put this three things together and a man is controlled to do whatever the controller articulates. In the USA we see a TV commercial with the image of a, semi naked good-looking woman promoting a car, a motorcycle, a beer, a razor, a place for entertainment, etc. We also notice that the social engineering projects of some governments invade these areas as if they were tools, then you would see people from the chosen racial groups or genders forming couples on TV news, soap operas, TV series, movies etc., or in commercial (propaganda) of any kind on billboards, trains, buses, etc. So, we can conclude that the country is under an intense hypnotherapy treatment. The general purpose of these groups used by *the invisible hands* is to manipulate our minds by making us familiarized with anything they want with the ulterior purpose of controlling our lives; from directing our attention towards a presidential candidate to deviating our attention towards the acceptance of any new unimaginable idea, whatever this would be, *power* again.

There are cultural suggestions conducted hypnotically through traditions, for example: A friend of mine, Wally, as a truck-driver instructor gave directions to a person who happened to be from the same country of origin as his, Afghanistan. He came to the USA at 5 years of age but still spoke his native language at a decent level and guided this individual without success for hours. Later, another person told Wally not to treat him equally, but to give him an order not an instruction, and after following such suggestions, he got successful results, immediately. This is a story taken from a direct source. These types of suggestions or methods of preparations to hypnosis are cultural and are deeper than the regular ones which are commonly called *memes*, word introduced by [11]**Richard Dawkins**, which are ideas originated from a strong but invisible source; basic unit of ideas for imitation with a similar concept of the biological gene compared with a mental string of information called, Meme, commonly transmitted from person to person, but also used by some interested group with some particular purpose of creating an idea about a product, a government candidate, a destructive conceptual idea, to lie about a tax, to rumor, to discredit, etc. Examples: 1- Apple computer is better than any other computer. 2- The ABC candidate will exterminate all people of the green race. 3- The reptilian people are our friends, they do not want to kill those people who are not reptilian like them. 4- Jesus died at 100 years of age. 5- Recent excavations prove that Jesus' tomb is in RDQL City. 5- Cannibalism is a normal behavior and it has to be respected or receive penal retributions. 6- Love others just the way they are since they are unique. 7- If those thoughts come from the Eastern continents, they are better than ours.

EGO

Ego is simply the transformed body of the mind which can be affected directly by the soul when this is filled with evil. Or, in other words, *ego* is the face of the mind when the soul contains mostly evil. Then, the mind operates accordingly with the content of the soul. If the soul is filled with evil, the mind

---

[11] **Clinton Richard Dawkins** (born 26 March 1941) is an English ethologist, evolutionary biologist and author. He is an emeritus fellow of New College, Oxford, and was the University of Oxford's Professor for Public Understanding of Science from 1995 until 2008.

Dawkins first came to prominence with his 1976 book *The Selfish Gene*, which popularized the gene-center view of evolution and introduced the term *meme*

thinks evil things, producing negative ideas charged with bad intentions that, after executed by our body, our *ego* also grows in strength. Contrary, if the soul is filled with the spirit, the mind thinks good things, producing positive ideas charged with good intentions toward people, animals and things that, after executed, beget the *consciousness* which is the opposite of *ego*.

The flow of energy comes from nature, the universe, God. Imagine a long string attached to your soul from the existence of God; you are pending from God above the earth as it was previously explained. We are constantly fed with good energy making our soul grow towards sainthood, but if that line is disrupted by sin, then we are attached to earth and our energy supplier is the king of earth, Lucifer. Here our *ego* needs to grow bigger, so it privileges money, possessions and finally power. The way our *ego* operates is by reacting with hatred. It does not have patience any longer, it becomes furtively dangerous to others, using the form of a mask called rancor, which in turn becomes even more subtle and takes the forms of frustration, resentment, disillusion, deception, depression, sadness, negativity, loath, abhorrence, abomination, execration, detestation; then, we have a major problem because we do not accept that we have been possessed by something opposite to God and we create excuses, pretexts, justifications for feeling something so bad as hatred incarnated into us, so we fake our presence as good in the eyes of the public, because a real *demon* does not want to be detected since it knows that being furtive, hidden and low profiled is being more effective to infiltrate in our minds. Then, *ego* becomes the person who does negative things based on negative thoughts, hurting people with more things of that kind. When people with big egos make a decision, they defend it no matter how wrong it is. That is why when this kind of people select a presidential candidate, they can be killed for their priceless decision because it was made by those who can never be wrong. Ego is right in its own opinion. Ego takes the face of a new demon, the recipient's one.

SIN

Sin is the falling action that a compulsion in us dictates us to execute mentally or physically (Romans 7:23). Sinning is the way by which our actions create some negative energy that feeds the demons that reside in our soul. Temptation is the tool with which the food in the form of sin is picked up and nurtured to the evil mind. We can sin by reacting in response to some internal or external stimuli with the additive of pure hatred or in its disguised forms as ire, upset, disappointment, resentment, rancor, frustration, indignity, fury, etc. When we sin we declare ourselves in rebellion with God and in harmony with Satan, so we reject the goodness coming from us or from others. It is as if we immediately formed part of the opposite team and we, consequently, get affected accordingly by the things that either group accepts or rejects as their own. Example, once we sin, we form part the group of wrong-doers, feeling comfortable with the wrong actions coming from us or from others. We would be advocates of the wrong things like lies, indecencies, infidelities, and of the wrong doings in general, thus, you would associate with people who practice the same activities and think the same way as you. This is when you decide to vote for the wrong candidates, those who use corruption to obtain their will and do their egocentric actions to appeal to your egocentric mind; those who produce laws designed to fulfill their benefit without considering the consequences to other lives or the destruction of other's property. The first step to avoid sinning, is to accept that sinning is wrong; the second step is, sinning no more (Saint John 8). This is like realizing that we are lost, because if we do not realize it, we would still continue entering into unknown realms towards our oblivion.

We would be accused of being sinners because we judge; however, we need to evaluate things and people in order to continue existing in a safe environment; we need to live a balanced life between the physical world and the invisible world. How is it that you are not going to appraise that someone has any kind of bad intentions against you; to steal money from your business, for example? What if someone plans to invade your house and kill you? We need to see how things and people appear to our senses; by looking and identifying the suspect (profiling) we are not sinning yet, because condemnation is the sin, so if we see others without hatred, resentment or any of those mask-hating tools, we are not judging. We are only practicing our capacity of observing things in front of our eyes and comparing them with our natural instincts or with their description on the sacred books where all the manifestations of the human heart are shown, with its frailties and its strengths after being overlaid against each other. Some people are afraid of making decisions based on their feelings against their enemies. You have the moral obligation to defend yourself and your family. If your actions are in self-defense, so you are not sinning. If you see what is in front of your eyes, you are not under the dominion of sin. Example, if you see a thief and you know it is a thief because he is stealing, you are not judging the existence of a thief. You are acknowledging him. You just treat him as what he is, nothing less or more than that. We do not judge when we believe our eyes and ears, we only recognize that he is a threat to our belongings, but if we did judge him for it by hating him, then we would become part of the group of the opposite leader, the Satan's itself, not part of the group of God. In such case we only needed to nullify him if it were possible and give the rest to the proper forces, forgetting the case from your heart, after that.

SIN BASED ON NATURE

The word sin is synonym of disobedience or rebellion against our creator.

1. Water. This element is the essence of life and according to the Bible, this element does not appear in the list of creation as if it were the representation of God himself on earth, and when water is ignored and treated with disdain, it can be wrongly replaced by any other substance, as in the case of alcohol when we use it with the intention of indulging ourselves into pleasure, refuge or to escape from reality.

2. Air. Oxygen is one element that is contained in both, air and water, and it is also treated with disdain and often used by inhaling substances to strike our ego with constant stimuli like smoking tobacco or any other similar substances with the intention of indulging ourselves into pleasure, refuge or to escape from reality.

3. Food. This essential medium to life preservation is also treated with disdain either by the anorexic and bulimic people or with adoration by glutton individuals; while one group rejects food, the other group accepts it with no limits in a form of entertainment or salvation replacing God. We also use it with the intention of indulging ourselves into pleasure, refuge or to escape from reality.

4. Sex. This reproduction medium is often treated with ignorance and consequently abused as a way of hitting our ego in a form of entertainment or salvation replacing God, also with the intention of indulging ourselves into pleasure, refuge or to escape from reality.

Water is the main element in life. Without it, we die. Since our beginning, we are water. The fetus is 98% water, a newborn is 90% water, and an adult is at least 75% water. This means that whatever changes occur to water, the same changes happen in our physical bodies.

The properties of water had been unknown for thousands of years, but scientific investigations conducted in Russia and Japan have given us important contributions about our understanding of this precious element of life, which in turn, extend our understanding of humans, physically.

According to [12]**Masaru Emoto**, water has memory of itself (you can expand your information about him and other scientists by visiting www.beyondbelief.com with George Noory, radio personality of Coast to Coast AM) which can retain the energy from the people around it, changing its molecular formation consisting in a hexagon. This hexagon-based formation changes with any external influence forming a unique figure each time it is stimulated. Based on these changes, the matter that contains this water also changes from decomposition to affluence. The same results occur in animals and humans, manifested in more variables like sick or healthy. We conclude that if our body is formed of water, also our water contained in our body charges with any external influence, consequently, by the consumption of any energized water one is being energized equally. No matter the type of energy of the water, positive or negative, this energy is transmitted to all the human organs, equally. This relates to the reason why Jesus Christ taught us to pray for

---

[12] **Masaru Emoto** (July 22, 1943 – October 17, 2014) was a Japanese author, researcher and entrepreneur, who claimed that human consciousness has an effect on the molecular structure of water. Emoto'sMa conjecture evolved over the years, and his early work explored his belief that water could react to positive thoughts and words, and that polluted water could be cleaned through prayer and positive visualization.

the food and liquids we consume. Since food contains water getting into a world made mostly of water, it will synchronize with the same atmosphere of positive energy, thus providing the expected benefit to our body, guiding it to a good health. If we influence the water in ourselves and on others, maybe we can collectively influence on the oceans and rivers, giving us healthier water for the consumption of all of us.

The previous bases for the purpose of sinning are all with the objective of indulging our ego with pleasure but also to avoid reality, escaping or entertaining our soul with some energy higher than ours.

GRATITUDE

[13]**Lorraine Day** has a very controversial life experience, especially when she had cancer in 1991 when she refused to receive a treatment based in chemotherapy, radiation and operations, the same way that she had administered herself to many patients in her professional practice as a surgeon at The San Francisco General Hospital, where she noticed that people died after such interventions, be she could do nothing; however, this time it was personal so she could disagree with it. She battled against cancer and defeated it in a very unpopular manner, she used faith instead of the advanced treatment known to society at that time, decision that also invited many ill-intentioned

---

[13] **Lorraine Jeanette Day** (July 24, 1937) is former orthopedic trauma surgeon and Chief of Orthopedic Surgery at San Francisco General Hospital and promoter of alternative cancer treatments.

She first became controversial when she began advocating that patients be tested for AIDS prior to surgery. In recent years she has promoted an alternative cancer treatment program, which has attracted criticism as being "misleading" and "dangerous".

physicians who discredited her ideas relentlessly, but it was worth because it meant her life; she would be dead if she had followed the advice of her family (who just believed in the medical society for years), friends and the pressure of her co-workers. What she did was very inspiring to many people, given that against everyone's opinion, the only chance she had then, was to put herself under the hands of humans. She practiced a very strict diet and prayed daily to recuperate her strength by stimulating her immune system. She used the uncommon common sense to battle cancer. Her opinion about the causes of cancer include malnutrition, dehydration and stress. Her dramatically painful way to suffer culminates in an emotional way of successful experience when she listened to her intuition to put her case under God's hands and for that, she is grateful, being this action, one of eleven points of her recommendations to defeat cancer. Another important point is diet; for many of us this means a sacrifice, which is one way of touching humility like people of the past did. People offer God their sacrifices with intentions to receive economical compensations by giving their money to the church. Few people really offer something real from themselves; their only real possessions are their sacrifices in the way of fasting and by ending their vices, but only if they are expecting health and happiness. Some other people only receive satisfaction for following the law of God by doing the right thing, and for that they are gratified, in peace.

I watched two of her videos "Cancer Doesn't Scare Me Anymore!" and "You Can't Improve on God!" When Lorraine felt grateful about her condition and when she strived for her life, she sent positive vibrations to the water in her body providing energy directly to it and, in this way, contributing to her survival. I was simply impressed by all the information she provided in so short time in her videos. If you wanted to see for yourself and expand your knowledge about this special case, you can inquire at her company ITV Direct, Inc., P.O. Box 7083 Beverly, MA 01915 @ 800-558-4846.

SLAVERY

For millennia, mentally strong people dominated mentally weak but physically stronger groups. In the beginning smarter tribes dominated others for hunting and later for building huts and monuments. Smarter groups paradoxically needed protection from other tribes and needed to govern other surrounding groups for the simple fact of survival. The ancient Egyptians, the Chinese, the Indians, the Greeks, the Romans, the Africans and the Native Americans were cultures that based on slavery for their working forces and militia. In conclusion, strong-minded people dominated physically strong people for their taxes or for their physical working force. It was not until some individuals with higher consciousness on the oppressor's side, realized that this practice was inhumane and did something about it, with the final result of its abolition. The oppressor's mind knew how to manipulate the masses and dominated the oppressed for the same purposes and reasons that we, in our modern times of high technology, are basically dominated. For the intension of gaining Power, *the invisible hands,* existing from the beginning of history, have dominated entire societies and have exerted their relentless forces to influence wars, controlled economies, switching kingdoms, dosing technologies, used slaves and created new versions of slavery. All above mentioned topics are tools to these powerful minds because wars are necessary to them for the acquisition of lands and to establish their machinery for the production of supplies for the new necessities created by their own needs. These wars provide the necessity to employ new workers as the movement that occurred during WWII when the women population had to be incorporated to the working force of the land to replace the previous line of workers (men) who was fighting against our enemies. This move doubled the working force capacity, causing the wages down by half when the war ended, in benefit to the secret groups, of course. Later, the right leaders had to be elected to help the continuance of the benefits that the war offered. Technology had to be measured since without any economic benefit, did not make sense to let it become public, that was the sad case of the genius scientist Nicola Tesla who invented the alternate-current method of transporting electricity (to mention only one of dozens of equally important of his inventions) to the benefit of society, also he invented a method to provide energy to the whole world via wireless using his World Power System. The secret groups with the little help of *the invisible hands* stopped the project declaring Tesla mentally incompetent and put him aside, to live in a luxurious hotel, where he was existing, but unable to create (because it was not profitable to the secret groups) more inventions to improve the life of the public.

The modern slavery is maintained by the use of the right chosen political candidate, the one that offers the public an easy way of life. Those politicians who can incentivize the public with negative emotions that frustrate, irritate, excite, infuriate, satisfy, and oppose one group of people, dividing the public. In other words those politicians who inject negative emotions to the masses and who engaged them emotionally, they will control the masses, but the control must be invisible and in minute changes, using the old-well-known principle of the frog under the boiling water. After this step is completed, emotional slavery is ready to be delivered.

Physical slavery has been eradicated in the world, even though some people disagree about this fact for their own self-enrichment purposes, following the same principles of manipulation for the obtainment of power that demons pursue. Now we have a more sophisticated slavery, which is the invisible one above mentioned. Before, the slaves were only some groups that molded this class, now everybody is slave somehow. The general public first, because we succumb before the subliminal propaganda of product consumption expanded through all the media as [14]**Edward L. Bernays,** who was a [15]**Sigmund Freud**'s nephew, started in the early 1920's. Then, the owners of big lands, the owners of media production, *the invisible hands* groups, who used this principles in an organized manner for the purpose of obtaining power, also succumb to the relentless need of power to nurture their huge egos formed in their souls filled up with evil that converts them in demons. In other words, the suppressors also became victims of their own methods of suppression and manipulation, becoming lower in the stratification of the demon environment. Let us remember that demons need to consume negative energy to survive. So, my call is for all, even for those who think they have everything, but they forget that they need *love* to descend to the valley of peace and happiness. All of us are slaves who have to identify those forces that keep us in that slavery condition to eradicate them for good. Let us start by observing the shackles of mental

---

[14] **Edward Louis James Bernays** (November 22, 1891 – March 9, 1995) was an Austrian-American pioneer in the field of public relations and propaganda, referred to in his obituary as "the father of public relations". He combined the ideas of Gustave Le Bon and Wilfred Trotter on crowd psychology with the psychoanalytical ideas of his uncle, Sigmund Freud.

[15] **Sigmund Freud (*FROYD*;** born **Sigismund S. Freud**; 6 May 1856 – 23 September 1939) was an Austrian neurologist and the founder of psychoanalysis, a clinical method for treating psychopathology through dialogue between a patient and a psychoanalyst. Freud was born to Galician Jewish parents in the Moravian town of Freiberg, in the Austro-Hungarian Empire. He qualified as a doctor of medicine in 1881 at the University of Vienna. Upon completing his habilitation in 1885, he was appointed a docent in neuropathology and became an affiliated professor in 1902. Freud lived and worked in Vienna, having set up his clinical practice there in 1886. In 1938 Freud left Austria to escape the Nazis. He died in exile in the United Kingdom in 1939.

slavery. These are the habits that become compulsive forces that push us to consume substances or unnecessary products to keep us in the state of slavery, provoking us into escapism in the form of vices in all of their dimensions. Hate and its derivatives are the main media of a mental fetters and shackles that keep us attached to an idea, thing or person especially when we reject it compulsively. The problem occurs when we add negative emotions, in any of its forms, to our actions. The hidden mechanism of compulsory triggers, guide us to the wrong attraction, making us something that we do not want to be, even when we realize that while doing the wrong thing we are in sin, but we end up doing it anyways (Romans 7: 15-20). Let us do what Jesus Christ instructed us in the only prayer for us to repeat. He said "to forgive the people who offended us, and to not let us fall into temptation..." This praying passage helps us to become free of revenge, free of hatred, because "hating is like drinking poison with the idea of hurting the hated person" paraphrased from the Bible. In reality, by hating, we sin by creating an emotional bonding between the hated person and the hateful one. This bondage is stronger than any physical chain which destroys us internally instead of affecting just externally, by the way, it will have its effects in the physical also. Example: If a man slaps his wife, she suffers the physical pain once it happens, but if she remembers the scene with hatred, even 50 years later, she would be re-feeling and re-enforcing the same act again and again as if it that scene were really happening again. At that time the reaction of hatred has created a mental fetter, a mental bond between the man (the aggressor) and her (the slave), his actions with the emotional element (mental chains) are what makes that past action into slavery. Do you want to get rid of your emotional shackles? "Get rid of your hate against your offenders" as Jesus Christ said according to Saint Mathew 5:38. If that woman gets away from her man physically, does nothing if she remembers his actions with hatred. His action will be attached with mental shackles in her mind until she releases this feeling or until she dies. This mental bonding will set her to attract other man with similar characteristics with her unconscious intentions to revenge her sufferings from the actions of the previous man; it does not matter that the new man is innocent, in her unconscious mind, all men are equal, originating the hatred towards humanity. The other extreme would be to attract people with opposite characteristics of her previous man, which in turn, would remind him again, creating a new problem on top of the original one, just for not resolving her case of hatred with forgiveness from the beginning. And the curse of their lives continues creating new and more complicate problems like depression, anxiety, and stress to them and to society in general. This is a case of common slavery. So Jesus said "Forgive your oppressor and you will be free".

LOVE

We think of love what we were taught by civilization, through tradition, changing from one generation to the next; from just loving the people of my group to loving everyone in the mode of "I love you just the way you are", theme by [16]**Billy Joel**, as if it were a yoyo emotion. But while love is one of the most difficult feelings to define as all simple things are, it is the easiest commodity for people holding innocence in their heart like children. For some religious people it is easier to describe by saying that love is God in the form of a man called Jesus Christ. But for those who are not religious its description through other feelings would be my next probable approach to do it, so love is the positive energy that makes a person

---

[16] **William Martin** "**Billy**" **Joel** (born May 9, 1949) is an American pianist, singer-songwriter and composer. Since releasing his first hit song, "Piano Man", in 1973, Joel has become the sixth best-selling recording artist and the third best-selling solo artist in the United States

patient, kind, happy, without hate, humble, without pride. Love does not insist on its own way; it does not rejoice at wrong but rejoices in the right; it endures all things; it never ends (fragments from 1 Corinthians 13). But this kind of love resides only in the ideal people—some of the readers may be part of this group—because it needs to emerge from a pure soul. The love we have for our family is in the direction to this cycle and the love from a mother (she is in a spiritual phase at this time) to her children is even closer in comparison, resonating at a higher frequency. The love many of us have for a spouse starts as infatuation that sometimes converts later into real love. Love does not need to be recognized as love, because it is love. The love that the world knows is based on the wrong rules because it accepts whatever the definition tacitly defined by the media, at that moment. The media are the group of manipulators that define love when it is beneficial to the ones who dictate to them from a hidden pedestal of an unknown location. They are one of the heads controlled by *the invisible hands* that show the masses the direction and the forms of our love or hate. Love from the world perspective starts with a feeling that escalates from admiration (the beauty, elegance, intelligence, etc.) towards respect; then towards infatuation, in other words, we confuse love with our feelings of the *I want, I desire or I-me-mine* modalities. Situations vary according to opinions depending on how far from the uncommon-ideal human we are, for example, a thief, a party lobbyist, a terrorist elevates their prayers to their god before they steal, lie or kill their next victim who was tagged as a victim in the name of love for his family, political party or god. In this case there is a feeling of closeness but with the negative energy, which proves not to be the real love. Love does not destroy or kill for pleasure or for revenge, but love can defend its core of the loved ones when necessary because it does it without hate, just to preserve his or her life and the lives of the loved ones. In this case, love is capable of killing another person when it is forced to choose between the lives of the loved ones and the aggressor's life. Here still, love does not rejoice for the end of another life, just because the human body is the creation of God and for it, needs to be admired, respected and protected. We would be short in our efforts to compare ourselves to the love of Jesus, because as a human being, he did not defend himself from dying, instead he offered his life in sacrifice to show us how to live our lives the best way possible through loving God, teaching us how to become dignified through being grateful to the creator of our lives by forgiving those who offend us. When Jesus sacrificed his life for speaking the truth to the world, teaching us the way to the truth towards God, he became, for his actions and virtues, **the unit of love** to the world, because he is the only one; the highest level of human incarnation ever in the existing of humanity with the moral authority to declare these profound words: "I am the way, the truth and the life; no one comes to the Father, but by me" (Saint John 14: 6, 7) and for that reason he was accused, condemned and crucified for blasphemous—even to the present days. He meant that those who become like him, would have the spirit in their souls, being the only mobile to transcend towards the father's realms. So, he offered the truth, for us to accept or reject his invitation to imitate him. He did not defend his life at that moment because his actions had a higher purpose for all of us in exchange for his life. Had he retracted from his words, he would have saved his life, but with no meaning to us whatsoever, given that it was the way to teach us with the body of dignity to defend our convictions. Many people presently defame him and accuse him to be a liar, but to defame him would be innocuous, since just to be a liar the person automatically represents weakness and he had to be brave to let be killed for his convictions. To accuse him of craziness would also be harmless since no crazy person would know the scriptures to apply them so logically like he did. He had to have Love in his heart. Love for the world.

If the whole population of Jews had the same character of Jesus, the Romans would have had no grip against them, so they would have been saved from the yoke they wanted to free from, but those, like Judas, who were of the idea to save Israel from their physical oppressor, thought that Jesus was his people's physical savior; the warrior they were expecting for years. So, they did not understand his message, and apparently, attitudes do not change, since people in the present, mock the words of Jesus, falling in the same broad path of ideas of the past with the toys of the present, thinking that our salvation is procured by our physical entertainment through gadgets, sports, food, pornography, drugs, and things of the sort.

If we sacrifice ourselves for someone else no matter who this person is, we are actively loving in the name of God, with a unit of love compared to Christ's love, but let us remember that we are only an image of God, so we always are going to be short if we compare to him; however, this action would be enough to reach our goal to imitate Christ or in other words, being like him, and if that were our choice, that would be enough to become saints.

An example of false love is when parents give anything that their children demand. Here they are not teaching their children the path to real life where they will be facing common people with needs and ways to obtain what they want without scruples, in many cases. To restrain our children by disciplining them, does not mean not to love them, but to show them patience and perseverance to prepare them to live the real life. Sometimes parents compensate their lack of love to their children by giving gifts to them or by not correcting them at all, in this way, they are buying their acceptance. In this case, parents are being ego-centrists themselves, acting without love, and creating false connections with their children.

Love is the strongest force in the universe which vibrates at Alpha frequency, affecting anything, everything always. And the love of God is the most comfortable feeling of all. So, when we love God, we accept his decisions over us as natural physical beings and also as spiritual-capable entities; at this moment, we are in unison with nature and we are more likely to have a happy life. If we on the contrary, rebel from God by sinning, then we are in conflict with nature and most likely than not, we would have a conflicting life, which would push us up to reach for happiness in the wrong places like in the cities of the world, a beach, a house in the prairie, in girlfriends, boyfriends, friends in general; sometimes we look for happiness in things like cars, houses, collections of any kind of objects such as sport cards, stamps, toys, cars, art, shoes, sport caps, etc. without finding it, frustrating us more and pushing us the second time to look deeper into a more sophisticated distractions, refuges and escapism that in the end give us some temporary happiness in the form of pleasure, but again, without finding love. And this becomes an endless cycle that jumps form escape-refuge to condition to finally illness. It would be like disassembling a piano in the search for music.

Jesus showed us the secret of life in one simple idea: "love God by forgiving your offenders."

CHAPTER TWO

THE SOUL

The Soul is the ethereal body. It is like a container that can hold the evil or the spirit. The soul is the element that remains alive after we physically die, traveling somewhere in the universe to different dimensions. Some experiments made by Russian scientists in the past and in 1901 by the American scientist Duncan McDougal in regard to the weight of the soul after experimenting with tuberculosis patients. This experiment was conducted by placing the about-to-die individuals on a scale and observing their weight before and after their death; however, the conclusions are not totally convincing, but they indicate that the soul has a weight of about three-quarters of an ounce. Some scientists agree and some other disagree about this statement ending in an inconclusive validity; nevertheless, weightless or not, through our intuition, the soul is part of the human creation.

The Soul is the ethereal human being who uses a physical package form to become a thinking person, ideal or common. The nature of a human being cannot be detected through the common senses that we use in our three-dimensional world. If the soul is separated from the physical body it would return to live in another physical body (reincarnation) only if it is prepared for it, if not, it goes to a waiting period for another chance of learning that might occur in days or in eternities, before it has a chance to return to fill another physical body (1 Corinthians 15:44-46). The soul separated from the earthly body goes to another dimension to gather with different other souls of higher energy to help the arrangement for the next reincarnation with the purpose to experiment life (not necessary on earth) and in that manner to ascend at a higher ranking of souls. Then, the soul that occupied the body in a previous life is not the same as the person we knew on earth (1 Corinthians 15:51). It is only those souls that have not transcended to that level yet, for any reason, the ones that mediums claim to have access to. Those souls might have died accidentally or have some unsolved matters on earth that keep them from leaving completely, either to wait for the next already decided reincarnation or to plan for their next one to come. In other words, if the soul has transcended to the higher realm, so it is not in between this material life realm and its final destiny, limbo, it is unreachable. This idea makes it difficult to believe that some medium reach every single soul at any attempt because, let us say, if the soul has had several reincarnations, it would have to select the body with which it existed on earth and who was related to the one the medium is looking for. At this moment the soul is like a ball of fire, like the flame of a candle with no emotional attachments to any previous incarnation, just with the level of consciousness gained after spending those lives on earth as a human being.

The invisible body; the ethereal body of our being contains either of two elements: the spirit in the case of a saint or evil in the case of a demon or a combination of the two in the case of the common human. In the first case we experience the emerging of *love* and in the second case, the emerging of *hate*. In the common human we have a battle of dominance between these two forces which occurs hundreds of times daily, in other words we fluctuate or flip-flop between one and the other state. When our soul's predominant element is the spirit, we have a direct contact with God; here is where the contained element in it is love, giving the initiation or continuation of consciousness into our mind, and the first step to the journey of becoming a saint. When our soul predominant element is evil, we have a direct contact with Satan and the contained element in the soul is hate, giving the initiation or continuation of ego into our mind, and the first step to the journey of becoming a demon. In the common human there is a continuous fluctuation between consciousness and ego; that is why we are good with some (usually with our family, friends or some who we prejudice) and bad with others (usually with our enemies or with people we also prejudice)—either of these forces get into our soul through the mind but just as a guest, not as a dweller, until we decide which of the two forces will reside in it. This manifestation of uncertainty reveals the existence of a self-decision process to determine what dwells in the soul. That is the reason why we were created with a *free will*, otherwise we would be called robots instead. This isolated idea is why our relationship with God is like a *silver string* that connects us with him or the strong *gold pillar* that connects us with earth. Then the relationship God-human resembles a pendulum, swinging closer to good or closer to bad. Imagine a long string to your being from the existence of God, you are pending from God above the earth, this is when your predominant feeling is love—the falling angels were pending this way. When we sin, we disagree with God, we are in rebellion against him, then the communication with him is disrupted and we are subjected to the force of gravity from earth, in other words we are grounded, becoming like a metronome with a tick-tack of an earthy music; we are still in the same position but not pending yet, but supported from earth by a similar imaginary line sitting on a pedestal of gold that ascends as our ego grows, in this case separated from God, here your predominant feeling is hate. Generally, in the common human, the soul is seeking a point of balance jumping from evil to its opposite which is the spirit when we are undecided about which way we want to belong, both guests in the soul, making the human being eternally battling between good and bad with attempts to become an ideal human. It is not until we decide which way we want to go that our soul evolves in the direction of perfection or devolves in the direction of imperfection. This decision is difficult to make, because if it were so simple, so would be the answers to our problems which are the reasons why we are discussing them now. We have temptations, so we want to have the power of solving our own problems, but every time that we look for power, our ego becomes more important and grows while ascends as if reaching for God, but instead it reaches to a god-like condition, defeating our original purpose of solving our own problems. This is a proof that even at looking for our own solutions, we can be trapped into ourselves, looping spirally downward and sinking further into oblivion. So if we need answers, look for them with love which in turn manifests itself as patience in the realm of the physical world. We have to live our physical form, reflecting our mind in our ethereal body and vice versa.

The *soul* is energy, shaping the ethereal body like a container that can hold the evil essence or the spirit. The soul is the element that remains alive after we die, traveling somewhere in the universe through different dimensions or remaining in the same one.

The soul is the individual, but once it is attached to a body it becomes the human with all the historical data relevant to that particular being. This means that when the soul detaches from its human package at death and it is not in its original human environment, it continues to exist, not as it did in the body it left, but in a different form. If it traveled outside such environment, it became the original energy that previously decided to take the particular human shape in order to learn important development for its attunement, but containing all memories related to all its previous reincarnations.

THE BRAIN AND BODY

The brain is the organ, the hardware (the computer) that is operated by the mind (the software that identifies a person). The brain is the physical operations department, the upper part that directs the body. It weighs about 3 to 3½ pounds and contains about 15 billion of memory cells connected themselves by their dendrites (branches) to their synapses (joints). From the point of conception, the nervous system is formed within 21 days of gestation, then the brain starts developing for 14 days from that point. The gestation process completes the nervous system after 20 weeks of conception. A mystery for scientists is, if the number of neurons, calculated to be about 15 billion, we only use about 5% of them, processing about 3 billion stimuli when awake to 21 billion stimuli when engaged in severe activity and thinking, why do we need so many neurons? Obviously that we forgot how to use a higher percentage because we do not know how to apply it for out-of-body experiences, premonition, telepathy, teleportation, healing, mental kinetics, etc., but they are ready to be used. The brain weights about 2% of the total body weight; however, it consumes 20% of the total supply of oxygen and glucose in the bloodstream, after the system has processed minerals, vitamins, hormones, enzymes, glucagon, insulin, protein, carbohydrates, etc. On average, the heart pumps from 7 to 11 pints (1 pint = 473.176 milliliters) of blood over to 60,000 miles of arteries, veins and capillaries that reach the whole human body. This amount of blood contains an average of 25 trillion red cells plus 25 billion white cells. Red cells have an average life cycle of 120 days to carry oxygen and white cells have a life cycle of 12 hours to fight invasive organisms. The white-blood cells are the cells of the immune system (The immune system is composed of many organs in which the most voluminous are the colon, the splinter and the liver) that are involved in protecting our body from infection diseases and foreign invaders. Two thirds (66%) of the blood is water. During an average age, we breathe about 500 million times. A baby has 306 bones and an adult about 206 bones, with 650 muscles and over 100 joints. The average man has 20 square feet of waterproof skin with 4 million receptors in it to protect us from the elements. We consume about 50 tons of food and 11,000 gallons of water during a lifetime.

It is an attribute of the brain to vibrate at different frequencies or states, being four, the principal ones: Delta, Theta, Alpha and Beta waves.

Delta waves cover from 0.99 to 4 Hz. These frequencies occur at the moment of profound sleep. When we experience dreams, these low frequencies vary within its boundaries. Here is where out-of-body experiences may occur. Sleeping is the time when the brain restores itself, making the pertinent connections necessary to maintain a normal brain functioning. At this time, any emotional or psychological disturbance that occurred during the day or in a previous, conscious experience compensates itself in a form of a dream. This action repairs the damaged connections, the psychological traumas of the previous day so if it is not much to repair, then not much dreams are needed. The dreams are impulses from our brain or from unconscious mind or both that converge to a stage of reparation, so the brain translates them into images, sometimes not directly related to the real motive, giving origin to dream interpretations, decoding their images to ideas and meanings.

Theta waves cover from 4 to 7 Hz. This is the state in between awareness and sleepiness. This is when dreams, problem solving, new ideas, sparks of knowledge, etc., occur. Usually if we do not record the information obtained in this state, we forget it.

Alpha waves cover from 7 to 14 Hz. These frequencies are relaxing, passive, meditative, waves of the brain optimum to learning activities. Here is where we, if we were ready, can receive the lighting of God's energy. See the Meditation section in this chapter.

Beta waves cover from 14 to 140 Hz. These frequencies show at a normal conscious moments of daily life. Obviously this stage covers all of our intensities while we conduct our regular lives, with varieties going from happiness, extended to excitement, anxiety, fear, frustration, anger, hatred, depression, etc. Here is where our sub-conscious mind is written by intruders, disturbing our peace.

This mini-fact spark of information is just for us to know how complicated our body is and how grateful we should be to have it functioning in good health. If you checked the "Symbolism and Numbers" section of chapter four, you will find some curiosities in regard to numbers.

The brain enables humans to learn through all the sensorial capabilities presented to us, being the basic modes: visual, tangible, olfactory and auditory with combinations between them that educators have been using to teach billions of students around the world, for centuries. Obviously that memory can be triggered in many more ways and people like Edward L. Bernays knew about it, creating vast ways of influencing entire generations of people all over the world by just mere subliminal suggestions propagated successfully through radio, TV, newspapers, cinematography, memes, etc. Later, his methods were practiced by [17]**Adolf Hitler** through

---

[17] **Adolf Hitler** (Braunau, Austria 20 April 1889 – 30 April 1945) was a German politician who was the leader of the Nazi Party (*Nationalsozialistische Deutsche Arbeiterpartei*; NSDAP), Chancellor of Germany from 1933 to 1945, and Führer ("leader") of Nazi Germany from 1934 to 1945. As

his minister of propaganda, [18]**Paul Joseph Goebbels** to completely dominate the German population. In the present, big corporations spend billions of dollars to publicize their products through the entire media. Also, politicians who seek power or who are already in power use the same tactics to influence the public to favor their elections. If they did not know about the secrets of turning the opinion of the public through mental manipulations like suggestions, sublimation and hypnosis, they would not spend time, money and effort in this practice. They know that the mind is suggestible, hypnotizable to finally controllable. Few are the politicians who do not rehearse their moves in order to affect us with false ideas covered as good ones; few are real, but, in the background of their knowledge, people, through their intuition, perceive the real ones. Using these methods of publicity and propaganda, few people of power, dominate entire nations moving their attention from Beta to Theta, Delta or Alfa. In other words, we are kept unaware of reality through entertainment in the form of movies, sports, terrorism, pornography, music, religion, technology, etc. or by extreme work to keep the other group of skeptical people busy thinking about how to pay for the elevated prices of fuel, food, housing, etc. away from thinking about ourselves and our problems. These fluctuations of mood keep our hormonal levels unbalanced originating real illnesses or psychosomatic ones on entire populations. Hormones like adrenaline, serotonin and melatonin stimulate our pleasure center too frequently, putting

---

dictator of Nazi Germany, he initiated World War II in Europe with the invasion of Poland in September 1939 and was a central figure of the Holocaust.

[18] **Paul Joseph Goebbels** (29 October 1897 – 1 May 1945) was a German politician and Reich Minister of Propaganda in Nazi Germany from 1933 to 1945. One of Adolf Hitler's close associates and most devoted followers, he was known for his skills in public speaking and his deep and virulent antisemitism, which led to his supporting the extermination of the Jews in the Holocaust.

it out of control. Melatonin is the hormone that stimulates the body to keep us sleep at night. This is converted into the *pineal gland* from its form as *serotonin* which is a hormone that keeps us alert during the day by reacting to the sunlight. When we eat too much carbohydrates, alcohol or sugar, we may be suffering from a reaction of an external stimulus that triggers our system to balance a low-serotonin level. The brain sends a message to the liver to release more insulin. This unbalanced hormonal level creates sicknesses of its own, for which we visit a doctor who prescribes legal drugs to cure these problems— to hide the symptoms only, I should have said—causing some severe side effects that create more imbalances that finally lead to operations in general, more sickness, more visits to the doctor, etc. This scenario is explained in the writings by [19]**Diana Schwarzbein** and [20]**Nancy Deville**.—At least that stimulates the economy, the politicians might think.

BRAIN EXERCISE ONE

When I was a young man, I believed for many years that I had a poor memory and to improve, I thought it was impossible. Well, as you know, if you believe something about yourself, that becomes true. In 1981 I found a way that changed my mind with great impact, and it was the method written by [21]**Robert Montgomery.** His great method changed my destiny since I was thinking about a way how to improve my memory, but

---

[19] **Diana Schwarzbein** is the founded of the Endocrinology Institute of Santa Barbara, California in 1993. She specializes in metabolic healing, metabolism, diabetes, osteoporosis, menopause and thyroid conditions.

[20] **Nancy Deville** is a coauthor of numerous bestselling health books, including Tire of Being Tired. She lives in Santa Barbara, California.

[21] **Robert Montgomery** an international speaker and trainer on sales, memory, public speaking, listening and motivation. www.learninc.com.

when I found this man, I did not need to reinvent the wheel in this area, just to follow his method.

Paraphrasing his method in his book "A Great Memory", consists on putting images to a list of numbers between 1 to 100 forming a block like a mental box, then to attach an image or idea that you decided to remember to each number and idea of the mental box, commingle them into a quick story that could come to mind easily. Example of a mental box: 1-gun; 2-glue; 3-flying bird; 4-table (legs); 5-glove; 6-fix; 7-store (7-11); 8-ape; 9-canine; 10-pen.

The list is longer, but just for the example I just give you up to 10. Now, let us say that you have a list of things you are doing in your day off: You need to change the tires of your car, buy some paper for your printer; call your brother; take your wife's car for an oil-change; investigate about a charge in your bank account that you do not recognize. First put things you can do in the same area, together. Second attach numbers like this: 1-gun. Think about loudly firing your gun shutting to the middle of two very small tires, then put 2-glue them to some giants drops of oil on top of your wife's car then, you see a 3-bird, flying eagle dropping rims of paper on top of the bank 4-table legs that break for the weight of the tires, the car, the paper, so you need to call your brother from the bank to help you out with your problem.

THE PLEASURE CENTER

The pleasure center is a sector of the nervous system centralized in the spine and the limbic system that produces a variable state of ecstasies in animals and humans when a dose of adrenaline (a hormone secreted by adrenal gland, located on top of the kidneys)—it requires the amount of water of an Olympic

swimming pool to delude one drop of adrenaline completely—
is released in the bloodstream where it reaches every cell of our
body, affecting our build by unbalancing the hormone levels in
the whole body. The feeling of pleasure or simply the sensation
of wellbeing and comfort is used by some manipulators to
control the actions of the manipulated ones. Some experiments
using monkeys stimulated with minute electric charges to
the limbic system made some scientists conclude that these
reflexes are related to the compelling impulses that push
animals to do something or to obtain something in order to
remain in that stage of ecstasy—pleasure is the prize, pain is
the punishment—and for it, even in minor doses, animals do
something proportionally not equivalent, they might even die.
Since the base of our nervous system has the initial formation
that of an animal, their conclusion applies to humans also.
Once we react to some external stimulus in the form of a post-
hypnotic object (form, shape, word, figure, picture, emblem,
behavior, sound, color, etc.) we secrete a dose of adrenaline
that affects the pleasure area in our nervous system causing
us to feel good and anxious for the next repetitive experience,
where in many occasions its importance goes above elemental
necessities to our survival. This concept has been used by
some secret groups for generations and applied to the world
population to obtain some economic gain that conduce to
power gain and its conversion in the form of negative energy
to feed their evil soul. The soul-food is in the form of misery of
the masses and the catalyst used to obtain it is power.

In many occasions drugs are included to products in order
to keep people addicted to them assuring their effective
consumption. In the early 1900's one famous drink used an
additive into its formula to affect the mood of people who
drank it. The manufactures included cocaine in the drink so
people felt energized after its consumption, they also called
it as "a tale of cocaine" which later was called by its short

name well-known to the world. Nowadays the protection agencies related to control of substances prohibits these kind of ingredients, but manufactures, now more sophisticated, use imperceptible amounts of hormones and drugs to stimulate the consumers' appetite for them. Some of many hormones, besides drugs that are added to drinks, meat, poultry, perfumes, facial creams, toothpaste, soap, deodorant, sprays, ointments, etc., are Oxytocin, Vasopressin and Dopamine.

Oxytocin is called "the commitment neuromodulator" because when it is released, it reinforces bonding or attachment to someone bringing a calm, warm mood, increasing tender feelings, lowering our excitement. For example, in women, Oxytocin is release in her brain during labor and when breastfeeding her child. Vasopressin is a neuromodulator that makes a light attachment to persons and things. Vasopressin is released when he becomes a father, so the attachment it produces is not as strong as Oxytocin; however, this neuromodulator is released in men at a moment of engaging in the sex act. The whole purpose of adding fusions of substances to products is to create minuscule but multiple attachments to consumers because they become more addictive and more difficult to control.

Dopamine (DA) is a neurotransmitter that is released in the *pleasure center* of the nervous system to regulate body movement and emotional responses like attention, learning, reinforcement, pleasure. It makes us feel good and so it makes us look for more of this feeling. Low dopamine activity may be prone to addiction; dopamine deficiency shows in people with Parkinson's disease. The lack of dopamine also shows in people who take high risks in any activity, this cases are common in young people and in people with lack of love from their family circle or people with no family at all.

A neurotransmitter released in the synapses excites or inhibits neurons. A neuromodulator enhances or diminishes the effect in the synaptic connection.

Other suspected chemicals added to some products with the purpose to create some sort of dependency are:

Acetylcholine (Ach): Affects movement, learning and memory.

Endorphins: Provide relief from pain and feelings of pleasure and well-being.

Epinephrine: Affects metabolism of glucose, energy release during exercise.

GABA: Facilitates neural inhibition in the central nervous system.

Glutamate: Affects excitement.

Norepinephrine (NE): Affects eating, alertness, wakefulness.

Serotonin: Affects mood, sleep, appetite, impulsivity, aggression. This neurotransmitter is naturally produced in our brain in limited amounts.

In addition to the previous list, about a thousand drugs in almost-imperceptible minute amounts are known to be added to cigarettes, two of them are cocaine and powder. As many may know, cocaine is a drug that affects the nervous system by stimulating it to produce extra energy from the body cells in ways that you use today your own energy of tomorrow, as if you had an energy-credit card available as long as you can afford it. GMO (genetically modified organism) is another way that the *invisible hands* use to control populations by altering food. This application to organisms, alters the natural chemical formation of fruits, legumes, vegetables, corn, etc. with the purpose of growing them bigger at less cost. But the immediate results come to the stomachs of the consumers when they become sick after eating them. With bad food, more sickness, more visits to the hospital, more medicine, more consumption, more money into the system and more dependent people. At least stimulating the economy by creating jobs, a politician may think.

With the little help of these mood enhancers, our brain receives a reward in the form of pleasure every time we consume an X product or when we listen the same information X thousands times we remember the product that makes us happy. Repetition is essential for our brain to remember information and if it is reinforced without effort from our part, even better. That is why publicity is so expensive, for example, one minute of publicity in a major sport event can cost millions of dollars that companies pay without hesitation because they know its effectiveness over the brain of millions of people who may pay for these products. In essence, we do not imagine how our decision-making system has been invaded for centuries by *the invisible hands*. They make us consume any product (music, food, books, cars, cloths, drinks, etc.) or make us vote in favor or against any candidate for the presidency of a country; change your way of thinking about any idea, for example: going to war against any country; forget any atrocities perpetrated by any of their favorite functionaries; make you participate in any social-engineered program of theirs, etc. through the messages we get on radio, social networks, TV, newspapers, magazines, etc. (in order of importance). Until we understand that these influences affect our lives by tampering our way of thinking to obstruct the way we were created to make us independent, we will not stop slavery.

THE MIND

Little Joe is making sounds of disgorging caused by the discomfort of some long catheter into his mouth connecting his stomach to some kind of container made of glass placed on a metallic table. In front of him there are some silver sort of tools neatly organized on a table in a white bright cold room. The treatment he is just experiencing has being brutal from the beginning—specially for a six-year-old child—moreover, he does not have his mother, father or any family member with him in the room; he feels alone and overwhelmed by the surrounding people with masks, on white gowns displacing themselves in the room with indifferent body language. He is sitting on a medical bed among these nurses and doctors when one of them, holding a long needle slowly pierced it into his left side of his back to extract something in the form of yellowish-liquid matter with foam from his lungs. Ms. Barbera, one of the nurses assisting the doctor in this routine, breaks the atmosphere of indifferent professionalism and holds his shaking hands and shivering feeble physique to give him instructions to keep his body posture in a straight position to facilitate, somehow, this intervention forced on him. He perceives in her words a charge of apparent maternal love. Little Joe feels an immediate emotional attachment towards her and continues crying, but this time with less bitter taste in his tears. The experience passes and he is taken to rest his body and mind.

Little Joe woke up suddenly few hours later with a heavy and stinging pain in the left side of his back. He is laying on his belly with his hands under his chest. He is on his bed and he starts dealing with his pain as if it were a big green tyrannosaur that he attacks with a gun that he holds with his two hands and from which bullets are continuously spouting as red-and-yellow lines that emerge and disappear silently in a splash after they hit its target. It was little Joe's imaginary way of getting rid of his painful experience.

All these images with feelings, colors, pain, and sounds returned to Joe when a nurse asked him if he was afraid of needles while she held a syringe in her right hand waiting to get some blood sample from his left arm. Joe just mind-traveled and came back from his childhood into his present time in a nanosecond. He used his imagination to hide his present into something else, the same way when he was attacking that big green tyrannosaurs of pain as a little boy. He, as an adult, used his mind as a time-travel machine this time.

This jump from present time to past time happens automatically in the mind and we could or could not be aware of it when this connection is triggered, depending on how we like or dislike that particular experience. As in our previous example, little Joe used his mind to fight his illness: pleurisy—unwanted water deposited in protective peripheral membrane of the lungs. He fought his pain in a form of a game. Curious is that this kind of game was not even invented in 1956, as if he rescued remembrances from a previous life. From here he continued remembering things related to that particular scene transferring the past to his present life, to shift experiences where another type of memory will emerge, mixing in continuity with his present life. He had nightmares that came to him in a daily basis for years until they disappeared some night when he reached adolescence. In his nightmare he saw himself in a sort of spaceship, immobilized in a glass bulb from where he could see the stars. The sense of impotence terrorized him. Another frequent nightmare of his was where he appeared walking on a hard and dry soil with a black sky, similar to the pictures of the moon, where fine strings rubbed his collar and neck causing him a very acute and intense pain same as the one caused by a paper-cut between the fingers. This painful experience was the reason he fought his mother against going to sleep when he was a toddler. He wanted to be alert and awake all the time to avoid his nightmares. While still in the hospital, he woke up many times in the arms of Ms. Barbera, who comforted him with hugs and kisses that from one time on, became those of a lusty-common woman. He fell in love with this evil woman who cuddled him frequently at night for 10 eternal months. He was introduced to these realms when he was not prepared for them yet, given that he was just a child, making this adult young woman a child abuser who was never charged for her atrocities of stealing little Joe's innocence from his childhood, emotionally crippling him for a good time into his adulthood. Frequently, as a young man with a girlfriend, he was transported to these moments that he obstructed futilely, since they came back as if they were wild bees, stinging their hive intruder all over persistently until his obliteration. I explained to Joe how his memories were hunting him and how they would continue hunting him implacably until he did something about it. Once he did, it took him at least six months, before his problems disappeared for good.

The mind is like a program that contains the essence of the individuals fixating them by remembering and comparing past memories with the present time, projecting them to the future to plan for their following life. Our brain makes these calculations millions of times during the day comparing its present with its past, making calculations for the immediate second or near future. So we have a memory that holds our past in a recorder; some psychologists call this area the *subconscious mind*. Here we collect everything as it is, without any editing and it is held for ever until the person dies. These memories are kept only in the main memory of the soul which also records anything occurred in the mind and the body of the previous lives of ours, unless the present life were the first incarnation, we can call that the *supra-subconscious soul*. This feeds the *supra-consciousness* which is in the image of our creator. Humans were created in God's image, so it is notable that the image of something is not necessarily the exact replica of the original sample. If you see your reflection in a mirror, your left hand is your right hand in it and so on. Yes, we look like God, but we are not exactly like God, just an image, and like him, we are capable of doing things like God, our image, in different proportion, otherwise we would be gods ourselves, which this would happen until we learn our lessons, then we become closer to God's characteristics but in less intensity. So we have similar physiognomies within our origins. This means that we are capable of doing things like self-healing and healing others; levitate objects as in the construction of Egyptian pyramids which lifting from 2 to 40 tons at once was necessary. It could have been that a collective mental force of a number of people lifted these blocks from miles away, cut them and put them in place to form a pyramid. We know that with our technology is not possible to accomplish such project, much less with the technology of the Egyptians who were living in the *Stone Age*. So if they did not build the Egyptian pyramids, who did? Were the builders using their mind powers?

Sometimes we have access to a similar event from the past using our *unconscious mind*. We have some feelings, good or bad, about some simple experience in the present that somehow affects us without knowing why, but many of our experiences have a connection with the past, either our own or through another person or vicariously, etc. Sometimes we do not remember the reasons for such feelings. If we portray the time element as a horizontal plane, just for the example, and our personal presence as a sphere, touching this surface at one point, and in motion on a straightforward direction. The point of contact between these two objects would be comparable to the present time. Our *subconscious mind* is like a recorder, following the point of contact on another flat surface but parallel underneath the time plane. Let us see an example: you find yourself in a dark afternoon showing the sky as if it were ready to rain, you walk on the streets and you feel sad, but do not know why. Your mind sends a message of searching for recognition to the *unconscious mind* which directs the routine identifying a dark sky, so the searching goes first to the short-term memory bank, if no information found, then it goes to the long-term memory bank, if nothing is found, the search is sent to the *subconscious mind* but it takes too long. When the information is found, it is sent to the surface to the *conscious mind* where it is processed, but just because it was too late, you just do not know the reason why, getting affected by your past, by the subconscious mind. If the information is not found in the subconscious mind, then the search jumps to the information collected even on a previous life of yours. The synchronicity with our present memory is missing. The *conscious mind* is not reached on time because the information was hidden too deep and the time factor is too fast in these areas, but what is true is that our present mind has been affected somehow. This effect can be observed by the wrong person and could be used as a tool to sell products or to plant a post-hypnotic order of some kind, example: when we see an advertisement on TV that brings us a happy moment from the past in which we were having a good time is because the common factors are used frequently, as when we are in a party with music, laughs, etc. This short glitch can be used by *the invisible hands* to sell a product or an idea with the intention to manipulate our decision process subliminally. Buying a product this way is only beneficial to the seller. Sometimes the idea is to convince people to vote for a chosen a presidential candidate, the manipulator would use the most effective medium, a TV commercial involving members of a chosen targeted people in mind mingling with each other, very happy and surrounded by comfort of a rich environment. With a background of music—when this medium is used by the wrong minds, it can cause serious damage to the minds of millions of people because they are writing to their *subconscious mind*, directly—with lyrics expressing the objective with its direct purpose. The message needs to repeat in cycles of seven. After this sequence is complete, part of the information is deleted and re-transmitted, so the subject tries to remember the message unconsciously by filling in the blanks. After this cycle ends, then another new message is sent, so the subject is never alone to think about his own ideas. Remember that it must be sent constantly until the listener, recognizes it as true. This process is not detected by our physical senses, but it is used to implant information directly in our *subconscious mind,* where it is detected and recorded. In this way its execution is undetectable by the person and when some related ideas emerge, they are treated as original. This is the way how we get hypnotized. We think that just by being awake, we are not subjects of these kind of attacks but the real thing is that we are controlled subjects to these manipulators so we must realize that we are under control, so we must observe the intentions of the *seed-planter* before letting him throw his seed on a fertile soil, your *subconscious mind.*

The principles are the same as explained above being the applications the only variants of the hypnotic method. The case of selling a product is very common. The seller knows that if he presents it to the public frequently on TV, radio, internet, etc. it will be sold. As consumers, we understand that we need the product, but how do we select it from 10 possible selections of the same kind that would satisfy our necessity? The seller who has the most money would expose it as many times as necessary to present it to the buyer as the most popular, and consequently, sell it. So, the frequency of information is necessary for it to be absorbed by the buyer's mind as good. For this reason, in these kind of product selling, this method is very frequently used by those who can afford it. This tool is misused by any person who, with any wrong motive such as evil compulsive reasons, takes advantage of others in negative ways which conduct to negative results like fear, deception, misery, depression or things of this kind over one or many people with the final purpose of creating emotional food for his evil soul or the soul of other demons of the same kind. These tools are also used by evil politicians who evoke to our egos to make us believe that who we are following is the right person. Once the idea is infiltrated into the mind of the voter through this method, using the evil support in his soul, he will protect his decision as if it were his own because its ego-centrist selfishness cannot be wrong. Ego is infallible in his own opinion. The recipients have to be of the same kind of the suggestion-maker ideas, who in their mind, they are making a decision using their free will. To prepare those people for such blind acceptance, first, the voters need to be corrupted by making them believe they are important, so they receive favors of any kind with the worm of entitlement. Their egocentrism needs to be pumped-up first, once they feel important enough, their ego is nurtured to make them feel even bigger. For example, politicians offer the constituents food-stamps, cell phones, free housing, affirmative action, pro-abortion laws, political correctness, free driver license, amnesty to illegal immigrants, low sentencing for crimes, free-gender-change operations, etc. In this way, big corporations and politicians, orchestrated by—do not forget them—*the invisible hands* write their will in the mind of the public by accessing their souls first. It comes to mind that the "serpent" did the same thing in "the garden of Eden", so the same story repeats itself, daily, again and again. Both perpetrators, the suggestion maker and the receiver are dealing with the evil-essence people who operate their minds, by orders of the dweller in their souls. Here we have a battle between the interests of a country against the interest of an individual. Here is where history has reported big atrocities perpetrated by one person against many just for nurturing the dweller of the soul at that particular moment of their decision. Examples: in [22]**The Battle of Thermopylae**, the Spartan betrayer against his country, Greece, informing the Persians invaders about a secret way to the back-site of the Spartan soldiers, resulting in the killing of the 300 heroic Spartans in 480 BC; the case of [23]**Marcus Junius Brutus** who laddered a betrayal conspiracy to kill his uncle [24]**Julius Caesar**,

---

[22] The **Battle of Thermopylae** was fought between an alliance of Greek city-states, led by King Leonidas of Sparta, and the Persian Empire of Xerxes I over the course of three days, during the second Persian invasion of Greece. It took place simultaneously with the naval battle at Artemisium, in August or September 480 BC, at the narrow coastal pass of Thermopylae ("The Hot Gates"). The Persian invasion was a delayed response to the defeat of the first Persian invasion of Greece, which had been ended by the Athenian victory at the Battle of Marathon in 490 BC. Xerxes had amassed a huge army and navy, and set out to conquer all of Greece. The Athenian general Themistocles had proposed that the allied Greeks block the advance of the Persian army at the pass of Thermopylae, and simultaneously block the Persian navy at the Straits of Artemisium.

[23] **Marcus Junius Brutus** (June 85 BC -23 October 42 BC), often referred to as Brutus, was a politician of the late Roman Republic. After being adopted by his uncle he used the name Quintus Servilius Caepio Brutus, but eventually returned to using his original name. He is best known in modern times for taking a leading role in the assassination of Julius Caesar.

[24] **Gaius Julius Caesar** (13 July 100 BC – 15 March 44 BC), known as **Julius Caesar**, was a Roman politician, general, and notable author of Latin prose. He played a critical role in the events that led to the demise of the Roman Republic and the rise of the Roman Empire. In 60 BC, Caesar, Crassus, and Pompey formed a political alliance that dominated Roman politics for several years. Their attempts to amass power through populist tactics were opposed by the conservative ruling class within the Roman Senate, among them Cato the Younger with the frequent support of Cicero. Caesar's victories in the Gallic Wars, completed by 51 BC, extended Rome's territory to the English Channel and the Rhine. Caesar became the first Roman general to cross both when he built a bridge across the Rhine and conducted the first invasion of Britain.

Emperor of Rome in 44 BC; the case of [25]**Benedict Arnold**, the American general who fought with the British instead of the American resistance; the case of the bombing of Pearl Harbor by Japan, known by [26]**Franklin D. Roosevelt** prior to this attack, without him doing anything to avoid it just for the purpose of engaging his country into the WWII, causing the dramatic death and wounding of over 3,000 soldiers and civilians on December 7, 1941. The Ford Company selling engines to the enemies, the Germans, during WWII in 1943. All cases, without any remorse from its perpetrators, done only for their self-benefit of grandiosity, vengeance or greed.

Let us remember that the objective is to connect our idea to a bigger picture through memory, reaction, change in our behavior, in our present or in our future sometimes based on our history or the lies about our history. The mind is the laboratory where all the thoughts are processed, studied and experienced before they are sent to the production line to be

---

[25] **Benedict Arnold** (January 14, 1741 [O.S. January 3, 1740] – June 14, 1801) was a general during the American Revolutionary War who originally fought for the American Continental Army but defected to the British Army;

[26] **Franklin Delano Roosevelt** (January 30, 1882 – April 12, 1945), commonly known as **FDR**, was an American statesman and political leader who served as the 32nd President of the United States, from 1933 to 1945. A Democrat, he won a record four presidential elections and dominated his party after 1932 as a central figure in world events during the mid-20th century, leading the United States during a time of worldwide economic depression and total war. His program for relief, recovery and reform, known as the New Deal, involved a great expansion of the role of the federal government in the economy. As a dominant leader of the Democratic Party, he built the New Deal Coalition that brought together and united labor unions, big city machines, white ethnics, African Americans, and rural white Southerners in support of the party. The Coalition significantly realigned American politics after 1932, creating the Fifth Party System and defining American liberalism throughout the middle third of the 20th century.

executed. The scientist is the I-Me mind (not yet evil or spirit but a combination of both) and his manager is the soul who at the same time has a CEO (chief executive officer) which are the *consciousness*, the *ego* or a combination of both (at the precise decision moment, there is only one that governs it), who deals with the board of directors that makes a decision to go with the *spirit* or with *evil* before a democratic vote or dictatorial decision that resolves which way to go, good or bad. Once the decision is made, your influence is absorbed from the constitution of your soul and executed by your physical body.

Since we are familiarized with computers more than anything else, let us use the computer format as an example given that the main idea to manufacture them was taken from the biology of the brain. First, the brain is a biological mass similar to the conformation of a CPU (central-processing unit), RAM (random-access memory for executing programs to avail the user), ROM (read-only memory for information to just process necessary routines for proper functioning) and the regular hard disk SSD (Solid State Drive) which is a block of empty space that collects information in the memory banks. The mind is what makes little Joe a little boy and that can compare with a program application in progress using software in a computer which utilizes the RAM to make it work. When we open an application we are the user of a product which might contain a name and a body with some information for whatever purpose. And if we put this program in the content of a robot with capabilities to substantiate itself with thoughts of its own for self-preservation, we have a similar way to the idea of how the human being is molded. self-preservation, survival, is the most instinctive information that a living cell possesses, created to defend a mind, ideas and a body in the case of human or just their existence any other organism like an animal, a microbe or a tree. All share one element embedded in them at conception, all want to live.

The brain is operated by the identity reflected in the mind, *I-Me mind*, using the *analytical area* of the one who identifies as the self who contains the name of the conforming identity who dwells under a combination of *ego* and *consciousness* in the soul. It uses the brain mechanisms, accessing all its components like the *short-term memory bank*, the *long-term memory bank* with its subdivisions in it; the *unconscious mind* where the *automatic mind* operates, which contains part of the *reactive defense mechanism zone* (reaction against excessive emotions of fear, pain and joy producing cry of laugh), the *operational sector* (breathing, peristaltic motion, endocrine balance, heart beat and all the organic functioning) and the *instinctive mind* (survival, reproduction) which is the *core mind*, the zone that can be compared with the BIOS (basic-input-output-system) of a motherboard of any computer where all the basic info is needed to start a computer running all the procedures, automatically (rebooting). Here we hold our more basic instincts to speak in general terms. These different areas work in unison to support the mind of a human being. All this information is not taken from any existing book, but I just place it in a manner that I can convey it to others comparing it with some existing psychology books. This information is in the *cosmic library*—so to speak—which can be accessed by intuition in similar ways that the late American Psychic [27]**Edgar Casey** did in a deeper manner. These practice came against him when he had his body energy negatively affected resulting in his death. Some of us just meditate and pray; he did it by a sort of mental medium activity called "readings" that only few

---

[27] **Edgar Cayce** (March 18, 1877 – January 3, 1945) was an American Christian mystic who answered questions on subjects as varied as healing, reincarnation, wars, Atlantis, and future events while in a trance. A biographer gave him the nickname, "The Sleeping Prophet." A nonprofit organization, the Association for Research and Enlightenment, was founded to facilitate the study of Cayce's work. A hospital and a university were also established.

known people in the history of human life have performed. Casey had a way of deeply communication with the existing energy of the universe but he disregarded how to just get this information from the *cosmic library*, his body consumed energy instead of just obtaining it. His "readings" were like self-sacrificing events to him. He was one of the great pioneers in conquering the human mind starting with conquering some of our human paradigms about the limits of the mind.

The awareness of the mind as [28]**Carlos Castaneda** referred to the self-awareness in his book "The Teaching of Don Juan", by finding a place where one could feel mentally safe. His observations included some natural drugs like Peyote as an enhancer to access the *conscious mind*. We can refer to the *conscious mind* as a horizontal surface in continuous motion interrupted only when we sleep or when we pass out; we are like a heavy sphere touching the flat surface representing time as mentioned above. This is the moment of our present time when we feel, day-dream, desire, act, and react to all aspects of life, knowingly, day by day. Here we use the brain and some of its peripheral components to communicate with our surroundings.

We sort with our memory all kinds of decisions that life presents us every moment in contact with the world. Example: When we drive our vehicle we need to know who we are; where we are going; what we are going to do; the rules of traffic; how to drive

---

[28] **Carlos Castaneda** (December 25, 1925–April 27, 1998) was an American author with a Ph.D. in anthropology. Starting with *The Teachings of Don Juan* in 1968, Castaneda wrote a series of books that describe his training in shamanism, particularly a group that he called the Toltec. The books, narrated in the first person, relate his experiences under the tutelage of a Yaqui "Man of Knowledge" named Don Juan Matus. His 12 books have sold more than 28 million copies in 17 languages. Critics have suggested that they are works of fiction; supporters claim the books are either true or at least valuable works of philosophy and descriptions of practices which enable an increased awareness.

and so on. These are some of the minimum information we need to know at the present time to solve a simple problem of displacing somehow from point A to point B. Now, if we had a concern of any kind that it is bothering us while we are driving, In order to sort it, we would need the *short-term memory*, the *long-term memory* and the *analytical area* in the *unconscious mind* to solve it while we drive using the *automatic mode*. In many activities of life we are physically present but mentally in another place or time, where we do not even remember how we got to the place you become conscious.

The *short-term memory* is section of the *memory bank* where we recently deposited some info about ourselves, someone else or something which can be retrievable immediately but that can be forgotten easily unless it is moved to the *long-term memory* by repetition or emotion. Example: The daily news; the name of something that we would like to retain on purpose but it does not have enough emotional impact on us or we do not repeat enough to being retained. However, this info is recorded in the *subconscious mind*.

The *long-term memory* is the section of the *memory bank* where we keep some info but where we deposited it to retrieve after moments or years in the future. Example: The name of someone or something; an experience of any kind, etc. These concepts, even though simple, are necessary for viewing other concepts that can be related to observe, but which are intuitively understood with no much emphasis in the form of words, just feelings. Also this info is recorded in the *subconscious mind*. This kind of memory is also deposited in the cell outside the brain, so it can be accessed immediately, this is where the computer designer took his inspiration from to design the *cache memory*.

The mind is the interface between our soul and our world that based on its essence, takes its lists of codes to form ideas to execute them within its body and the outside. It is like a computer program for which we locate ourselves amongst our surroundings and the tool that allows us to coexist as an active part of the whole scenario.

WILL-POWER & SELF-CONTROL

Will-power is the forceful action of the mind that provides some energy to the body for doing or not doing anything with the purpose of obtaining a desired result, beneficial or not. This action is applied at the mental level using logic as an enforcer, causing a secondary effect problem because it is a decision deposited in the brain, without transcending to the unconscious mind. This kind of information is deposited in the cell memory. Example: some people make personal resolutions the first days of the year, commonly, knowing that when keeping them, the results would be favorable to them as in the case of a compulsive drinker who realizes that stopping this activity would bring him good changes to his economic reality and to his relationship with his family members and friends. He is using logic here, but one week after his promise, he finds himself drinking again. If will-power is used to learn a discipline, you learn it and you obtain benefits from this effort, but commonly this kind of learning leave people in an indecisive level retention, never reaching the complete retention level; that is the reason why you see a great number of people in the fields of art, religion, computers, engineering, communications, etc. performing at mediocre or average level, but occasionally you see a so-called genius—because geniuses love their occupation, they become so imbibed into their field reaching a level of proficiency not needing any will-power to be that good. Will-power dissipates high amounts of energy derived from some internal organ, leaving us tired or exhausted. Obviously, you become tired with the need to recuperate your energy somehow.

Self-control is when the same previous scenario occurs, but this time with a different approach, this time the person realizes the effects of any action or habit from another angle, he sees himself doing bad things, making bad decisions while under the behavior of observation, understanding the damage he does to himself in different areas of his existence, at this moment of realization, he is convinced, repented and ready to make changes, not before. Once you control yourself this way, you have conquered your ego, yourself by knowing that your conduct is opposed to the one defined by God. This power is not yours; this is God's power. If you claim this power as yours, then you have ego in your soul competing and rebelling against God. With this method, we activate our natural energy with understanding and conviction, letting the energy of God work in us.

BRAIN EXERCISE TWO

Using your brain-alarm clock is a very useful tool that activates your neurons and prepares them for more related brain self-programming. Let us say that you wanted to wake up at 6:21 the next day. Before you sleep (already in bed), first, think about that particular time in big red numbers, tilting with high intensity. Second, give your brain an order to wake you up at that particular time. Third, forget about it and close your eyes. If it does not work, try it until it does. It would take you at least 7 days in the worst case, but it will happen.

This exercise will prepare your brain to more activity of this kind and it will make you more aware of yourself and your surroundings. You can use it for any kind of clock related situations, once you have been successful with the original exercise.

POWER

Power is the final objective to the human being who has evil in his soul; the negative-energy-food machine of Satan; the stimulus that this negative entity needs to keep itself alive. When some individuals cause pain, fear, despair, frustration, disillusion, fury, resentment, indignity, disappointment, ire, unhappiness, depression, trauma, anxiety, stress, etc. onto others, they get remunerated with pleasure, satisfaction and subsequent temporary-false happiness, that is why they are never satisfied with what they obtain; they are looking for the next ecstasy moment equal to that first one that caused that extraordinary excitement in the same manner that the first drink gave many of us when we were young; the first drug experience; the first time traveling, the first car, the first emotion, etc.

The search for pure power is when the soul has been invaded by evil already and it is ready to mutate to some other higher level of demon. This change happens also in the brain. This change is why some scientists conclude about the plasticity of the brain explained in the book "The Brain that Changes Itself" by [29]**Norman Doidge**. The soul is only waiting to grow itself with its new resident in it and that is why it needs to be nurtured using cruelty and terror over other people, obtained through power. Here the mind operates without any struggle, it just simply performs whatever thought crosses its realms of control. These are the individuals—the power users—who possess billions, even trillions of dollars for them to use, but who still need to meet some deadlines to complete a financial

---

[29] **Norman Doidge** is a Canadian-born psychiatrist, psychoanalyst, and author of *The Brain That Changes Itself* (2007) and *The Brain's Way of Healing* (2015). *The Brain That Changes Itself* describes some of the latest developments in neuroscience, and became a *New York Times* and international bestseller.

objective. They do not need money, they need to dictate, to feel important, to dominate, to fulfill a necessity in their inner self, their soul, to gain the emotional food needed for their continuance. They are people who have to get their companies to a highest level of achievement, who want to please their own ego. Some of these individuals and their families could, each one of them, spend one million dollars a day without extenuating their resources for over one hundred years. This can give you an impression of how rich some of these people are, giving us an alarming idea why do they feel compelled to pressure others to get more money that they do not need. They need the feeling of importance coming from an outside observer, because they are insignificant inside if compared to the uncommon-ideal man. They are unhappy inside and they cannot find the real fulfillment of happiness, but they think that feeling happy is the same as being happy, so they look for that feeling, day after day, year after year. When the next year, the cost of living increases 4% for the regular population, for the emotional-food grower people the increment of importance must also be 4%. We have to have 4% more money to physically survive, they need 4% more ego importance to survive egotistically. While the majority of common people will never be rich to feel happy, the majority of rich people will never be happy for they will not stop searching for emotional food to nurture their souls. But both groups are looking for the same furtive objective, happiness, in the wrong places. For both groups is the same search for happiness, continually until the end of their time, but looking as if we were hamsters running in circles endlessly with empty-never-ending hopes, they are feeding their egos incessantly. The real happiness occurs only when we become free individuals. We would conquer ourselves by not conquering anything, but by not being conquered by anyone, or nothing else either.

Money and knowledge are stepping-stones to power. In many occasions we study for the wrong reasons. We get in areas where we know other people have obtained money and we think that we would be getting on their same path to reach our dreams, but we do it no matter the complications because our real objective is to be powerful. This simple motive in our way to happiness is empty, I do not mean the results, because if you become a person with power and you exert it with grace, without pride, there is no sin about it. We sometimes even give and take things or money to get power. That is the case of some rotten politicians who get money in the form of donations to obtain power without any remorse of selling their own country because their purpose is above anything, their own soul included. When the people who donate money to politicians, do it to get some favors in return of their investment, their final objective is also to exert power. A man in many occasions invite a girl to a good restaurant or show himself very generous in front of her with the intention to get what he wants, power over her body; she on the other hand presents herself very passive and innocuous until she gets what she is looking for, power over his wallet. In other words, power is our main objective although our ways to get it, are many and very sophisticated, varying in form; they could be money, knowledge, influence, generosity, humbleness, innocence, etc.

Power is the finest delicacy to feed our ego because it contains negative energy to feed the demon in our soul. Once our soul predominantly contains this kind of energy, our mind is charged also in the same way creating negative ideas that convert themselves into bad actions or reactions. That is when we have many people in all areas of societies in front of us hating everybody, creating chaos among many of us. That is why we see politicians expressing words to defend our country while in reality, they do the opposite. That is why some leaders entice their own people into hating other groups creating division, portraying themselves as victims just for the purpose of getting power. They know how to trick our minds to obtain power. At that moment they are creating emotional food for their boss, Lucifer.

When we experience any of these negative feelings, we are deceived and think we have all the right to be mad, we justify our thoughts of revenge to punish the perpetrator, whoever or whatever they are or represent. We react this way, most of the times only in our mind, but with less frequency in real life. At this moment, we have a dilemma of possible consequences given that if we react violently towards the subject, we might get punished by society, but if we just punish the subject in the security of our mind, then we think safely because we are not exposed to external verdict; however, this action derives energy within our physical body guiding us to distraction, to vices, and later to illnesses, whether we physically react or not. And when we have accepted this condition, we have to justify it again and through this, we obtain satisfaction, subsequently pleasure, then compulsion to obtain it, which becomes the food of our evil nature that we already mentioned before. And as food in our physical bodies is consumed daily, our negative feeling called hatred is also consumed daily by our soul that, if it wants to survive, needs to find new sources of food daily to satisfy itself. That is why when our souls are filled with evil, we need to feed our evil nature by hurting others through criticism, condemning or doing any form of hurting, frequently, in similar manners in which we need to nurture our physical bodies. This is when the serial killer, to mention the negative extreme for reasons of explaining our case, goes back in the hunting to hurt his new victim. No matter if his previous was wild enough; the next experience has to be increasingly more intense. Ted Bundy—to mention a well-known notorious character—had problems originated in the way his family raised him; he had a detrimental childhood despite he had all what money could provide; his father and mother did not love him, but ignored him pushing him to the villains who showed him their version of Love. But he did not know that as a responsible human being, he should have realized that killing people was taking his rage in the wrong direction with the unconscious purpose of solving his own psychological problems. He had a good-looking appearance and enjoyed the acceptance from girls, but he had a revenge agenda, hidden even to himself. He hated his parents and did the opposite of what they expected from him, physically affecting his female targets to soothe his internal painful necessities with the purpose of obtaining power from the hate towards them. But his behavior increased in intensity, number and sophistication with a never-ending satisfaction. Remember that our soul, under these conditions, needs to be impressed with a higher emotion because this is like our first drink; we are looking for the first original emotional spike every time we drink, but we do not realize that we need more of the chosen substance the next time we try to encounter again that good feeling. You know the rest of the story.

The negative energy originated by the use of power is the reward we are looking for at the end of the job, the fuel that the demon residing in our soul needs to survive.

Power is the force that pushes us to execute our will that in the end would temporarily satisfy our thirst to feed our ego. Power is the finest delicacy that feeds our ego or our demon because it contains the negative energy needed to nurture it. Once our soul contains this kind of energy, our mind is charged also in the same way creating negative ideas that get converted in bad actions or reactions. People turn into thieves, serial killers, terrorists, bad professionals, bad politicians, etc., hating and creating chaos into society since by creating any kind of dependency we conduct our control over others. In this case when they deceive people, they are feeding their demon dwelling in their souls through the pain coming from the victims in general. Their ego grows faster when the energy they obtain from deceiving the masses because it is higher, becoming bigger demons faster to serve their god. Not forgetting to mention the activity these actions create in the people who reject such decisions with anger, with frustration, with emotional reactions, and imprinting their souls with negative energy that will be used subsequently to dominate them furthermore. Finally, Power is the force that triggers a negative reaction into the souls of others by dominating them without mercy, approved by the victim or not.

RETURNING TO OUR PATH

We, most commonly, hide our bad feelings and act with our most friendly personality in front of people, but if we disagree or are bothered by them, we castigate our aggressors, but only in our minds. Nevertheless, if we look deeply inside us, we are unhappy with this motion. We shall know that we secretly have practiced this routine since young adulthood, but it was necessary, otherwise we would be in conflict with others too frequently, making our life impossible to live; the important thing is that if we disagree with someone is because most of the time we are thinking about our own side, with egocentrism, feeling the poisonous hatred inside us, but we were not created this way. We were created to be happy and to live happily with our neighbors. Since we know or feel that this is not our natural state, what can we do to return to it? This does not mean that we should be tolerant in excess to the point of stupidity; this means that if we need to step up to the situation, we need to do it right, without hate, just by doing the necessary move to solve the problem without involving our soul. When we were children we did not know the world protocols, so we spoke our minds with truth in it. This was the moment of experimenting the world, where we realized that this strong forms to show our feeling were not recommendable for a non-conflictive life with our neighbors. We came to the fast solution of applying hypocrisy which is one form of our extreme behaviors, causing the same effect because the feeling is still there; the reaction is not manifested but its consequences they cause internal, negative compensations to our body. Then is when we need to know our truth and feel the necessity to return to our natural state, the normal state of the uncommon human-being. We did not learn any other way of conduct from our parents who corrected us with hatred when they delivered discipline to us. Hating others was self-destructive, but we ignored it because it was part of us, until life taught us that when we needed to protect us from others, we had to hide our feelings from them and do anything necessary to solve our problems while we had to motivate ourselves through hate, anger, rage. Anger is the key element here, the trigger, the negative emotional bond. That is how we learned how to hate our neighbor by dreaming our reality instead of confronting it; by having conversations in our minds designed to solve our conflicts with our counterpart. Consequently, we learned how to suffer by reacting inside us and acting outside ourselves as if nothing happened, but this is like a time bomb that is ready to explode inside us. From the time of our creation to the present, things have devolved inversely proportional in us, so the ride to finding our path is slow, so we need to be patient. We need to be aware of our position first, then to change our direction to return to our highway. For that, we need to prepare our mind for war without physical armament because our enemy is invisible, intangible. First, we have to unveil the arms of our enemy, in order to design ours. Second, we need to clarify our terrain and understand what forces we are fighting against, so we need to develop a fit mind, we need to exercise mentally to become stronger. To defend ourselves we need to recognize that the dwellers in our souls and the souls of others are demons. We can start from understanding our real nature. We were not created this way, but we are this way now. We need to annihilate the demon who resides in us soon, then the one that resides in our neighbor starting by showing our behavior to them, our response in the form of *forgiveness*. So, let us portray an elemental case: by understanding the mechanism of an insult and the development of it, after we are insulted. If someone insults you, you listen to it, you evaluate it: a) what is the meaning of it? b) Where is it coming from? c) It thrusts in (most of the times) or it bounces out. You do all that mentioned in a micro of an attosecond (10^{-18} of a second) and most of the times you are insulted because you accept the insult. Meaning, if the insult comes from a person who does not mean anything to you or if the insult is not true, you should not get offended. We have opened our inner-selves and reacted towards the executor because our ego is so huge, given that by the minimum attempt of an insult, it gets awaken with anger, so we answer with rage. What if we do not open our inner-selves and ignore it just because it is not true or because we do not care about the aggressor's importance or because we are not going to waste energy in anything stupid like that? An insult is successful when it penetrates your defenses, exploding inside your mind when you react with hatred against it. This does not mean that you are letting anybody insult you, because you can stop the insults from its origin by not reacting or if responding, doing it without any hatred from your part, then the insult is nullified. Thus, recognize the context of the insult through your senses, but do not react, at this moment you can do two things, first proceed to respond, violently or passively, to the person who insulted you, return to your normal activity and forget about it. Second, do nothing about it and also, forget about it. Once we do this, the demon inside our soul does not get fed with our negative reaction. That is our purpose. Not to nurture the enemy that resides in our soul neither to wake up the one in others people's souls. In consequence, like any organism, if it is not nurture, it dies. At this moment we would have a good start to return naturally to our path like recurrent waters after the storm. If you practice the mental non-reaction response, either defending yourself or not, you would remain in your balance, contributing to your general wellbeing (Saint Mathew 5:38-48) "love your enemies, do not resist them…" Jesus meant, do not react to their aggression with rage because you play the demon's plan of hating back. Now, if we decide to exert some force, do it because it is your last recourse to defend your interest or because it is the only way that the enemy would understand, but without hate. When you do it this way, you are still practicing love to your neighbors as it is written in the scriptures, this time, with corrective love. This is what Jesus did when he aggressively ejected the merchants from the atrium of the church (Saint Mathew 21:12, 13), after that, he continued healing people with grace and candor.

If the last recourse is not doing anything because the other party is stronger than you and its attempt would finish your existence, then understand your position and accept it, but without hate. Once you practice this rule periodically in your life, the direction to your original state of mind is set the progressive count towards your origins, catching up naturally.

MIND EXERCISE ONE

To prepare our body for the reception of any message existing in our present dimension we can be aware of the *pineal gland* by just observing it. At the moment prior to sleep, elevate your vibrations of gratitude to God for your existence and then turn on your mental radar directing your attention to the *pineal gland* for approximately 21 seconds. If you do this for 7 nights before you start the meditation, your mind would be prepared for it by allowing you to stay focus on the intensity of the meditation itself.

PREPARATION TO MEDITATION

Some people might not know about what meditation is or what to expect from it. Explanations about this practice varies according to its origin since the idea of meditating just without any purpose would be like starting on a trip without a destiny. So it would be more beneficial to perceive it as if it were a tool that we could use with an objective in mind; it would have more perspective in a dimension designed to be objective. If the meditation approach were from the Far East, then its practices and benefits are very strict and difficult to know its purpose from the beginning, you would know its reason by yourself but until the end which might take years. Some people in the past accessed these practices and understood their purpose, thus provided an explanation for the public in general, so we could also benefit from this apparently insignificant, but important practice. If we think about meditation in a similar way as if we take our vehicle for a tune-up, it would give us an idea. It simply means to improve your mind by releasing it from stress and negativity, so it would generate more internal energy to communicate with other people, nature and God. Practicing meditation would amplify your perception, you would become aware of life making you more aware of your mind and your surroundings placing you on earth and in the universe at the same time by expanding your consciousness. The main idea is to prepare your soul to receive energy from the universe, from God. This energy may come to you in an infinitesimal amount but overwhelming to your body, since we are only a minuscule, invisible particle of this universe. The point of contact with the universe could be so short that compared it with the small enough moment of time between the sounds of our voice that travels to your ears be that of a ray of light traveling at the speed of 300,000 km/sec or 186,000 miles/sec for one year (a light-year), it would be so fast that the hearing of your voice would happen as if it would occur two days later, not in the present moment. Also, we do not know when we could be ready for this connection to happen (Saint Mathew 25: 13) "... watch then, because you do not know the day nor the hour when he will come...", only when it happens and after it has happened. All in all, you will be a better person the second after it happen given that your preparation has already provided you of the awareness necessary to awake your understanding of life, understanding yourself. For a more detailed explanation about the importance of breathing, you can listen to Anders Olsson's "Conscious Breathing". If you visited www.beyondbelief.com you would see him on an interview by Regina Meredith.

CHAPTER THREE

MEDITATION

Before meditating, find an isolated place where you can remain quietly for at least one hour without interruptions. Lit a candle, placing it at about 3 feet in front of you, concentrate in the form of the flame observing your thoughts at the moment of their emerging from somewhere in your brain. Realize that the flame is a physical example of the existence of life, because it consumes oxygen in order to produce energy itself. Do this for 7 minutes at the time with rests of 3 minutes, for three repetitions. This will give you the mental preparation to observe things around you, by making you more aware of yourself and your body. This is a warm up for the meditation. While still sitting, place your feet flat on the floor and your hands in a praying position close to your chest with your head forward inclined, prone to your hands. Close your eyes.

Start by breathing with inhalations in 7 seconds and exhalations (through your nose) in 14 seconds. For the unfamiliar person with this breathing modality start with 7 seconds exhalation but increase the lapse every time you meditate until you reach the 14 seconds, then your continue with this practice, but only when you feel comfortable doing it, without forcing it (or this will distract your practice).

Concentrate in your pineal gland thinking about it as the point where you will mentally take the mental flame to the middle of the cavity formed by your hands as if you were holding a ball of fire. Feel the intensity of the heat.

On an inhaling (7 seconds), mentally conduct the fire from your hands to your wrist, then exhaling to move the flame to your elbow, stop at the changing point and inhaling (and every time you get to a joint point); now at exhaling, conduct the fire to your shoulder. On the next inhaling, conduct the fire to your neck. On the next exhaling, conduct the fire to your right brain lobe; on the next inhaling, conduct the fire to jump to the left brain lobe. On the next exhaling, conduct the fire to your shoulder; on the next inhaling, conduct the fire to your elbow. On the next exhaling, conduct the fire back to the hollow of your hands.

The next step is almost the same, with the difference that this time you start on the tip made by your thumbs; complete the loop as explained previously and restart with the next tip made by your index fingers, complete the loop and restart with the next tip made by your middle fingers, complete the loop, this time with the tip made by your ring fingers, complete the loop, this time with the tip made by your pinky fingers, complete the loop going back to the hollow of your hands. All without forgetting the breathing rhythm. In the middle of each cycle, you will have a storm of thoughts coming into your mind; observe each one of them and quickly continue with your line of work, until another thought comes to your mind and do the same thing again and again with patience emanating from your soul. Do not mention a word or think about any answer as if you were mentally speaking, just observe everything. Given that you got the cycle, now you do it at your own pace, but the important thing is that you complete the loop every time you start it.

You can do this practice for 7 days at the time, then you skip one day and restart to complete another cycle of 7 days. After you complete three cycles, then you continue meditating without any stops until you desire. The meditation should be practiced once in the morning just after waking up and at night, just before going to sleep.

As a background sound you can use some meditating music that you can find on the internet or preferable you can use a small water fountain. The sound of water has a natural relaxation effect in our mind that soon would neutralize your anxiety and soothe your stress, transporting you to a calmed state of mind.

After the meditation, you can spend some time just quietly, without words in your mind. Just observing all the thoughts that now will emerge as if gulls over some abandoned food on a beach. But remember to omit words in your mind while letting yourself float on an endless waves of ideas, down the stream. Observe the flame on the candle you have in front of you and without any words in your mind, stop and finish this routine.

MEDITATION SECOND STAGE

Once you are familiar with the meditation practice, you could go to a guided meditation where you would have the opportunity of conducting your energy towards any organ in your body, to heal yourself; to get rid of any pain or just to energize your organs. Some people guide their energy to their heart, lungs, brain, kidneys, etc. while conducting the regular meditation, deviating their focus of attention from its original purpose. Reasons to believe that this kind of meditation is separated from the previous routine.

MEMORY OPERATION

In computers, memory is an electrical charge held by a minuscule magnet. This energy can be positive or negative like the energy in every single particle of nature formed by protons and electrons. This energy can be represented by ones and zeroes that when retrieved, depending on their order, can form a letter that combined with other letters can form a word, a number or an image that, when accessed, can be projected on a screen. This electrical charge in our brain can be retained also by some electrical charge in a brain-cell in a form of feelings, images, data, sounds or video including anything else recorded at that particular moment. The energy that imprints and holds this info permanently in our memory banks is triggered by positive or negative emotions. These emotions can be absorbed even by the pre-born child (fetus) through the mother's emotions, not by words at this stage; however, when the pre-born child listens the meaningless words, he or she does not understand anything, but words or information through the umbilical cord in the way of emotions get to his or her *subconscious mind*. Later in life when this words come to the surface as if they were bubbles urging to the upper level, they synchronize with whatever information has been recorded in the *subconscious mind* and at that moment of reality, the word or feeling gains a meaning as it pups up on the surface of consciousness, becoming part of the person's experience; this is the moment of instant knowledge that frequently comes to our mind without knowing its origin.

BRAIN EXERCISE THREE

It is very good exercise for your brain to put yourself in a very uncomfortable new task. This creates new connections in your brain keeping it active and tuned up.

Your task would be to write your name using your secondary-active hand. Later you will need to speed up the writing until you do it well as if it were your main hand.

Later you can extend your exercise further by learning another language. In both ways you will stimulate your brain cells in the same manner. The important objective is to avoid as many routines as possible, especially if you are a retired person, since you would tell your brain that your productive life has ended, then the brain-automatic process starts deleting unnecessary brain-cells connections, conduction to mental illnesses.

CONSCIOUSNESS & AWARENESS

Some people interchange the meaning of these stages of the mind, consciousness with awareness, but these words differ in meaning. Consciousness is our understanding from the soul point of view, about the realization of its existence with respect to the universe and the highest *consciousness*, God. While *awareness* is our understanding from the mind point of view, with respect to its surrounding physical world. Consciousness is the state of the soul that keeps us in contact with God and other people's souls. Awareness is a state of the mind that keeps us in contact with other people's minds, feelings and things in general. At this moment we can conclude that if we know who we are in the present time, then we are who we are, and not someone else. We have the awareness of ourselves as single living thinking creatures.

For many of us it is very difficult to keep our awareness in the present state for a long period of time. We need to do something that we call entertainment to feel in peace with ourselves, as if we are trying to escape from our reality. We watch TV, listen to music; talk with others and so on. Sometimes when we are alone and have nothing to veer off our attention from, we play music in our mind or have an imaginary conversation with some imaginary or real person also in our mind. Sometimes we create conjectures about this person, imagining opinions and scenes, and we respond to them with emotions as if they were present. Well, this is a common problem that takes place in our minds and which steals our happiness in front of us, because we need to get that entertainment that snatches our attention about ourselves in the present time. At this moment any exterior message is absorbed with ease. This is the moment when the *invisible hands* need to infiltrate our minds with their virus to later deposit any information of their choice. Here is where the *meme* (a mental information command for a person to accept as true and executed with compulsion—a post-hypnotic instruction) is formed to be proliferated ASAP. This can be similar to the virus in a person's body or in the operating system of a computer. In this case the idea proliferates to entire populations with the help of the media. Radio, TV, internet, all repeat the same idea to the selected population in order to change the way these people think about any product or idea, for example: who to vote for, what to think, how to think. Another example: a *meme* can be used to disseminate an idea with instructions of conduct directed to some areas of the population using some TV programs and movies where the characters are defined according to a selected sector of the population providing subliminal instructions for them to consume certain products. In the last ten years people feel like heroes for not smoking while in the past, this activity was very common because the media had dictated us to think that way. Another example of *meme* usage is to proliferate ideas to convince populations to accept the idea to start a war against another country. Obviously that the idea behind this primary one is that some producers can sell their tanks, airplanes, ammunitions, boots, gadgets, rifles, tires, food, cars, etc. After the WWII the production of all the previous mentioned goods increased to ways never seen in any society before, even the ways people behaved changed to benefit those who controlled the minds of the world, for example, women for the first time in the USA, formed part of the production force, placing the family to a second level of importance when children, since then, are not raised by their mother, but by a stranger. The main idea behind it was to increase the number of the working force by a multiple of two, and to decrease its value in half its price. We were not aware of the initial reasons, but the people finally realized it. The vast population is the last to be informed, but they are the ones who are real, because they trust the sentiments and motives of their leaders. The soldiers with their families are the ones who are real patriots for their sacrifices to make the necessary changes they are convinced to believe in—that is why I think that if wars had to happen, should be executed by the draft of every single person in all societies, not just people with economical necessities. But ideally, wars should not happen at all, because in the end, after millions lose their lives, limbs, families, peace, etc., only few, consciously, get the benefit of this tragic occurrence. The secret groups using their *invisible hands* unknowingly do something good when they create real feelings of patriotism in their victimized populations when they feel that their reasons to defend their country are real, because these are real people. They never suspect that someone economically benefits from others losing their lives. Here, the patriots are conscious of their love for their country, but they are not aware of the benefits the war creators are obtaining from their sacrifice.

INTERACTION OF HUMAN ELEMENTS

Any change in the three elements that shape the human being, affects proportionally the other two immediately because they are directly attached somehow, but the soul is the most important element of the three. The first impulse depends on the soul's nature before the mind starts operating. The body only executes what the mind dictates and sometimes, when the emotion is very intense, the body absorbs this information from the cell itself or the information from the spinal cord that keeps a copy of all the cell information once it has been established by repetition as a sport-exercise routine, for example. It is understood that when we have not committed to either one of the fillers (evil or spirit) of the soul for good, the communication between the three components of our existence contribute to each other, changing sides from good to bad and vice versa. But once we, somehow, decided for either one of them, this influence affects the rest more strongly, even changing our physicality making our brain plastic, so to speak as it is explained by Norman Doidge (cited in Power chapter) in his book "The Brain that Changes Itself", discovering that when a physical activity is adopted, the brain changes its structure, making new connections by its brain cells.

The *supra-consciousness* or simply God imprints humans with some basic information at the precise moment of conception, first, we have the input of the inspired necessity to connect with our Creator, the instinctive supreme being before us with whom we have to find a connection later in life. Second, we have the knowledge that if we decide to do something against (sin) our Creator, we are wrong, for that, we have a code of conduct written in our brain about the knowledge between good and bad, this is our capacity to develop our *consciousness*. Third, we have instincts of survival and of the preservation of the species. Humans have basic knowledge through inspirations about how to be humans, elements that establish our difference from other animals that only have basic instincts. We are animals in part for we share the same physical characteristics, sharing the information of the organic systems and its functions. For simple animals there is no much need to learn to be animals since their learning is a minimum selective behavior distinctive of each animal, and this is why the majority learn to survive by hunting. The lower the brain development of the animal, the more instinctive it is. A bee has more instincts proportionally in its behavior than a dog, while the amoeba has even more instincts than a bee. Another instinct is the preservation of the species. Some mammals teach their offspring some elemental behavior, necessary to nurture themselves independently, but when those simple instructions are not learned by an animal, the consequences are devastating, example: when a lion was born in a zoo and learned the zoo system (with all the training of how to conduct with humans and all their routines of feeding and cleaning) and for any reason it needed to be transported to its natural habitat; this animal with all the instincts and the looks of a lion, is not yet a lion, until it learns how to be one by experiencing life in the real habitat, nevertheless its appearance. In a higher scale, in similar ways humans look like humans, walk, speak, and procreate, but still need to pass the threshold to become at least common humans by learning the instructions from their creator. Because, first we need the preparation for independence to survive in the earth environment with lessons provided by both, father and mother. "The instruction of the father is a code, the word of the mother, a gospel" as [30]**Victor Hugo** wrote in his book *Les Miserables*. If we lack some of the experiences provided by our parents, we grow up with gaps in our character that in most cases, we never fill up, but we

---

[30] **Victor Marie Hugo** (26 February 1802 – 22 May 1885) was a French poet, novelist, and dramatist of the Romantic movement. He is considered one of the greatest and best-known French writers. In France, Hugo's literary fame comes first from his poetry and then from his novels and his dramatic achievements. Among many volumes of poetry, *Les Contemplations* and *La Légende des siècles* stand particularly high in critical esteem. Outside France, his best-known works are the novels *Les Misérables*, 1862, and *Notre-Dame de Paris*, 1831 (known in English as *The Hunchback of Notre-Dame*).

are ready to continue our experiences for we have the highest form of animal-cell combination on earth, platform necessary to receive the highest form of ethereal element, which is the soul that may contain the spirit or the ego, once we receive this privilege, we are obliged to discern the awareness of life and consequently, able to make good or bad decisions as human beings to accept or reject goodness or evil in our heart. Once we are aware of our lives, the next step is to develop our *consciousness* where we will decide to fill it with the *spirit* or with *evil*.

MIND EXERCISE TWO

Using the same place where you use for your meditation, get ready as if you were to meditate, adopt the same position, close your eyes, but this time, find the sport of your preference and mentally start playing it as if you were an expert, even if you never played that sport before. If you chose basketball, shut the basketball into the basket 7 times perfectly, no mistakes from an imaginary distance of 500 yards. Do 3 sets with 1 minute of rest in between. Use your imagination to change angles, distances and exercises. This will improve your concentration and will create new brain connections.

CHAPTER FOUR

SYMBOLISM AND NUMBERS

There is nothing magical about numbers just because they are numbers, but they have some meaning because they were used in our creation and they can be observed as obvious patterns in animal life, plants (flowers with a unique patterns of numbers of petals), sun, moon, seasons, etc. For example the evolution of creation on earth, symbolically portrayed in the Bible, has a reference of its creation in a multiple of the number 7, so this number is into our cells that we adopted the weeks with 7 days. Then the multiples of 7 like 21 have some attractions to many people, because they are considered as lucky numbers, but in reality they make us feel comfortable because they are everywhere in our DNA (Deoxyribonucleic Acid).

The 7 churches of Israel (Ephesus, Smyrna, Pergamum, Thyatira, Sardis, Philadelphia and Laodicea). The 7 Spirits of God (Apocalypse 4). The number 7 is obtained by the sum of other numbers frequently used in the Bible, 4 plus 3.The 4 horses of destruction (Apocalypse 5). Also the number 21 is equal to 3 times the number 7. The number 3 is used in the scriptures frequently, first in the trilogy of holy persons forming one God.

Jonas is swallowed by a big fish and remains in it 3 days and 3 nights. Jesus starts his apostolate at 30 and dies at 33. Jesus is crucified in a group of 3. Jesus resuscitated in 3 days. The number π (pie) is equal to 3.14 (7 x 2) plus infinite numbers (3.141592653589793...) representing the infinite omega. Jesus Christ resuscitated after 3 days after death (infinite). Mosses had a lifespan of 3 periods of 40 years, as a prince, slave and a prophet. The number 40 is more indirect since it is formed by 4 and 10–this is 1 plus the inclusion of the zero without altering the meaning of symbolism to any other number, just representing wholeness. The number zero, the block of nothingness, the beginning and the end, the alpha and the omega (Apocalypse 1:8). The trilogy is the perfect triangle, 3 times 7 equals 21 that represents spiritual body, so 21-1 is 20 or a triangle minus 1, which is the number that represents the common body. The number 20 is the physical body (a number of fatality, absence, destruction), 20 times 2 is equal to 40 an earthy number with mind and body but still without the Holy Spirit, multiplied 2 times equalizing an earthy man after eighty years of age before Moses' life purpose became complete, adding another 40 years to his life (as a prophet). The word quarantine means 40 earthy days of observation. Then the 40 days and 40 nights that Jesus remained in the desert, tempted by the earthy Satan, the god of the earthy things. 4 main corners of earth (north, south, east and west). 4 triangles of the pyramids (The pyramid Cheops is truncated at the top at the junctions of the 2 lines of each 4 triangles indicating the absence of a capstone that never was set in place as is said in Saint Mathew 21:42-44). 3 times 4 equals 12 apostles; 12 tribes of Israel. 4 archangels (Gabriel, Michael, Raphael, and Sariel). The 144,000 sealed people from the 12 tribes of Israel (12 times 12 plus 3 zeroes). And the number 13 which means the capstone of the pyramid if we relate the 12 apostles plus 1 (Christ) equal 13, who were 4 groups of earthy men represented by truncated triangles, until Jesus Christ converted it into 4 perfect triangles, being him the unification factor, the capstone of the pyramid.

Naturally the number one represents image for all things (a number multiplied or divided by one is the same number), so the number 1 is also very important; the unity of love (1 Saint John 4:8- 9) when in the body of a man (20) plus the unity (1) of love, adding 21 equal Jesus Christ.

BODY-MIND-SOUL CHANGES AFTER HATE

It is clear that the human energies transcend freely within the three different intertwined dimensions of the human nature which are: the soul, the mind and the body. So if good or bad is in our soul, this energy is transmitted to the mind generating feelings and ideas to be executed by the physical body and in the same manner if the stimulus started in the mind or in the body; it affects the other realms also.

Let us first see the changes that occur in the physical dimension when we hate. All the changes happen first at the electron level. When we get irritated, mad, emotional, resentful, furious, upset, hateful, etc. the adrenaline, norepinephrine and dopamine, powerful hormones that are part of the human body acute-stress response system are secreted into the bloodstream. They affect our body by stimulating the heart rate, shrinking blood vessels, and expanding our trachea and bronchia inflating and deflating our lungs during high stress or exciting circumstances, all of which work to upsurge blood flow to the muscles and oxygen to the lungs. When these hormones are forwarded into the blood stream from the adrenal glands located on top of the kidneys (about 3 inches or 7.6 cm in length), at least one of the electrons from the atoms that conform the cells of every organ of our body is replaced by one electron of these hormones, amplifying our energy, turning it more capable of executing (in a microsecond) reactions not commonly done under normal conditions--these natural self-doping boosters are reserved for the defense department. These reactions may cause us to run faster, jump higher, scream louder or to take higher risks, putting our life or the life of others in danger by acting irrationally, having uncontrollable body reactions designed to defend ourselves as part of our defense mechanism system. The feeling of power is evident, but when the effect of the intervening hormones ceases, the original electron forces itself to return to its natural orbit causing higher energy consumption to accomplish the electron displacement towards its original position. This energy is derived from somewhere in our body, usually the heart or the brain, even though, all organs contribute to this surge or energy usage, being the organ that released more energy, the one that suffers dysfunctions after long periods of stress and intense emotions; that is why we get cancer, heart attacks, strokes, etc. Some other minor effect is premature aging. Some frantic emotions in us can cause the same effect that hatred causes. We have the same experience, but in lower proportion, when we watch horror movies, gossip, judge, lie, steal, and when unnecessarily compete with others in any obsessive activity to accomplish anything. The reason is that we get addicted to adrenaline, and like any addiction, it needs to get performed repetitive times to get the expected stimuli until we become aware of the necessity to stop due to the anxiety, fear, obsession, overreaction, or any negative emotions that affect our health. This is the time when we detect any physical effects in our body like feeling our heart pounding irregularly, deep headache, chest pain, etc. these reactions force us to see a doctor. At that moment we are diagnosed with high blood pressure, heart problems, circulatory problems, digestive problems, insomnia, depression, anxiety, etc. Now we have to take medications that most of the time–being positive—end up with secondary effects more dangerous than the original symptoms. In essence, if we do not die, we live a miserable 30 last years of our life. But this should not happen to any of us.

This brings us to the point to seriously consider real tolerance in order to preserve our internal peace and consequently, our health. Sometimes it is unnecessary to overreact over any situation if it is not solving any or our problems at all. If reacting is a negative impulse, over-doing it is even worse because we use energy unnecessarily. In many occasions we keep quiet about any circumstance that bothers us, but we take the battle to a mental stadium where we, as if we were in the roman coliseum, castigate, insult, crucify, dismember, defeat, etc. our enemy causing us the waste of energy that we could have used in something productive. Sometimes we react to a just a simple imaginary idea formulated as a question formulated by anybody.

For example: John was absent at the hospital where Mary, his wife, was dying while her ex-husband visited for the last time. But when John knew that her ex-husband had been at the hospital he executed a complete scene of jealousy in front of the rest of the family and friends explaining actions about the next time he would see him around. He expressed with fury how he would have insulted him. Here Joseph extenuated his energy unnecessarily, because when John was present at Mary's funeral days later, Joseph did not say anything to him at all. So, it would have been better that he had conserved his energy for the real moment, not wasting his energy in trivial things.

Another real example: Michael and his family bought lottery tickets with a possible face value of millions of dollars, instead of waiting until the moment of reality and proceed, either with silence or with action, but without anger, when they had a routine reunion, they unexpectedly expressed their ideas about what they would do if any of them got the prize. All made plans about how to spend all that money and some of them even externalized their feelings about how much each of their present friends would receive, giving the supposed prize money to people according to their affection. After that reunion, they left with some remorse about what had transpired there. The next day neither of them got anything, but the bad feelings of the previous night still remained in each other minds. Here, all of them made the mistake of talking their minds and of unveiling their feelings towards each other for something unreal. The energy they spent was burnt already, leaving all of them with exhaustion and with hidden emotions externalized for nothing important, much less real. Let us be objective to use our energy in something real and use it when necessary. The problem is that when our mind gets negatively stimulated, the *sub-conscious mind* records everything and our soul gets also influenced by any negative feelings nurturing our ego once more, because the *sub-conscious mind* takes everything seriously, affecting the rest of our human realms, regardless if the facts were real or not; however, if they produced emotions, for the *sub-conscious mind*, they were real.

As it was mentioned above, some organs of ours generate the physical energy to be consumed at the moment of any negative emotion. Anger causes to excite our heart and lungs which need more oxygen to supply the demands that our cells urgently call for. If we get angry frequently, the flux of adrenaline and other hormones are secreted into our bloodstream more frequently, affecting the organs that supply this energy, also more frequently, which in turn need more energy to take from other organs to replenish more energy at the moment of relaxation which is when our body works once again to recuperate its normal condition, making us very tired. When this experience happens many times daily for extended periods of times, our cells become exhausted and the secreted wastes and pollutions known as toxins are not processed properly, forming undesirable deposits into random body locations, creating malformations in our cells that later are identified as tumors, cancer, lymphomas, etc.

These negative emotions like worrying, hating, wondering, stressing, doubting, overreacting, and more, create an unbalanced-hormone system that in turn originates psychosomatic and real illnesses in many people, most of the time. So we add fuel to the fire when we observe our surroundings and find an already damaged environment, economical disturbances like the high cost of housing, food, health care, and erroneously used social security money–which should be a personal, contributor account with interests paid, redeemable by the contributor only at certain advanced age, not as some extra income money taken by the government to pay those who exchange their personal integrity for their vote and who prefer not to work for living—creating problems caused or at least worsen by immoral governments that care more for themselves than for the people they were supposed to serve.

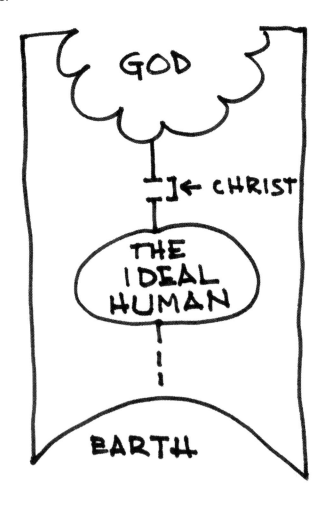

Real problems are happening to you in your mind at this moment when you read the depressive news daily, but instead of getting upset, relax your mind and think about the next time you vote, and decide to do it for those who will help to solve the problems of your country, not those of their own party. Relax and do something positive by not buying unnecessary things pressured by the necessity to escape from any bad experience. Instead entertain your mind by finding a peaceful scenario in your life and meditate. Some people use these moments of stress to dissipate their minds full of hatred or in its disguised forms as ire, upset, disappointment, resentment, rancor, frustration, indignity, fury which manifest in the form of hypocrisy, jealousy, corruption, immorality, pride, lavishness, injustice, degradation, aggressiveness, greed, gluttony, egocentrism, wickedness, avarice, infidelity, lust, impatience, xx-holism, sexual deviations, etc.; we usually do it by drinking alcohol, smoking, watching TV excessively, watching sports, etc. Then, when we vote to make changes in our surroundings, do it the moral way, in which you will be part of the solution, not part of your own health problems, given that they would affect your relationship with your family and friends, extending them to your community, to your country and in a long run, to the world.

MIND EXERCISE THREE

Once we refrain from doing the excess of something we like, we become more powerful, so start controlling yourself next time you wanted to eat or drink more than what you need by thinking about your self-control. If you start with a very insignificant thing you usually do, you will get some satisfaction; some people start with measuring their portions of food they consume. You will find uncomfortable at first because you would not feel to be yourself, but just observe your reactions—if you catch yourself reacting—when doing this experiment and catch yourself after the action of reacting. Plan your exercise for one week, then you move to something more important. But remember that you are not getting rid of things, just lowering its frequency or intensity. This is a mental preparation for taking self-authority over your process of selection, avoiding the chance for it to become a habit and subsequently a vice. Observe the mental process of desiring something to eat and not consuming it; then observe the mental process of doing it or not; last compare your feelings after the facts. Our main objective is to observe our behavior as if we were not ourselves; as if we were the drivers inside our own body.

BODY–MIND–SOUL CHANGES AFTER LOVE

When you physically respond (without reaction) to any external stimuli with patience, fairness and justice, you are reflecting the good spirit that you have in your soul. It means that you are pending with a silver string in contact with God. It means that the ruptured gap that existed between you and God before, has been repaired by the inclusion of the spirit of Christ. It means that the results of this important decision, are reflected in the abundance of life to you and your family. You present yourself to your neighbor with mental balance, honorable, humble, generous, forgiving, confident, strong, fair, committed, tolerant, dignified, cooperative, respectful, disciplined, organized, determined and happy. You are psychologically balanced to deal well with the injustices of society. You have faith and you are peaceful, you do not impose your will over your neighbors just because you do not think you are entitled to it; you provide an example of cleanness and dignity verbal or non-verbal behavior for all you do amongst all that surrounds you. Your soul generates a positive vibration to all your mind and body in tune with the harmony of the universe, becoming one with it; becoming one with God, walking towards perfection.

Your health improves because your soul sends good vibrations to your body to function in homogeneous harmony. Your mind gets the message from your soul that everything is working correctly and does not compensate with the intention to survive, for any imbalance perceived by it, so it generates positive thoughts enjoying happiness. Our desirable state of mind is permanent and continuous as if it were a flame supplied with the eternal fuel of goodness, emanating a refulgent, dazzling aura. This is our optimum state of mind, happiness.

FINAL PERSPECTIVE

The process of a thinking performed by the mind is energized by the force contained in the soul. If the soul is mainly evil, your thoughts will be bad and your actions will reflected, will also be bad, designed to cause pain and disgrace into your life and into the life of others. Pain, sadness, disgrace are few negative feelings produced by hatred in the invisible form of negative vibrations emanating from the perpetrator's soul, which in turn produces the food from which the resident demon in our soul needs to remain alive and growing until it becomes Satan itself, its final destiny.

When we do not know how these energies operate, we refuge in escapism or entertainments of any kind to get rid of the stress that these pressures exert over us. We need to keep our mind occupied by working harder, watching more sports, movies, pornography, food, alcohol, defining new gender deviations of any kind, collecting goods, purchasing unnecessary things, imbibing in drugs, etc.

Lucifer is the one who owns the strings of the Antichrist and its puppets. He is the one who plays those puppets with its *invisible hands*, making all of them believe that they are the originators of their own ideas and designs for their own future, but they are simply demons who follow their master's demands to be in harmony with his agenda of terror and misery. They are in synchronicity with their master Lucifer (Satan, The Prince of Darkness) hence they lie, corrupt, dominate, intimidate, revenge, procrastinate, violate, deceive, disturb, aggravate, enslave, terrorize, degenerate, etc. We see the faces of these demons daily in our regular interactions with people, on the streets, the freeways, at work, at school, on the news, at home, in the government, even at church. Also we see them on the faces of some who want to direct the future of our country and in those who lie to us in search for our vote. Let us be very careful when we see their apparent innocuous faces with a big smile and with their list of promises designed to exchange with us for our support because their demon is appealing to our own demon. Let us be careful about our own responses when we think of our own benefit and not the benefit of our country. Let us observe our own reactions; our own demon jumping inside us with happiness when we are tempted to do the wrong thing. Let us remember that those who benefit the most, have more power when they control the mind of the masses. They use the media in all its forms to manipulate, defame, and denigrate to be able to hypnotize the multitudes just because their master is lurking around, instructing them what to do next. In that way, the obtained power that even brakes some iron minded individuals to form part of their forces, produces the food their god demands. Terror, fear, sadness, disgrace is the food that produces the negative energy that their master needs to be happy in his own realm, the planet earth.

When we hate back, we become one of them, serving, in that way, the master opposite to God. That is why we must not fight against hate with hate. Because corrective love is necessary against hate in the form of discipline, patience and force but without any negative emotion, mainly without hate. In few words, the answer is love.

The puppets, mentioned in the beginning, moved by the strings operated by the *invisible hands*, think that they are acting on their own, but they are also used, because they are the Satan's energy collectors. Lately, we have been facing some kind of different enemies in the world that are more difficult to defend from, given that the cowards do not use conventional uniforms just the uniforms of their bad, wrong and evil actions. To fight them, we have to know their strength, first. Their weaknesses second. We do not need to argue with them, just to know their objectives. We do not need to understand their reasons, just to know their strategies. We should not try to proliferate their insults to the public. Their vocabulary does not have to be repeated because that gives them importance. They are like the regular criminal, when they employ all their power over their victim, but when the victims defend themselves and have them under their feet, they become cowards. Our objective should be to defend our country at all cost, but when we get them into custody, do not respect their customs at all. Do the opposite of what they expect from us, law-abiding people, to let them learn from the consequences of their choice, discouraging, in that way, future volunteers and copycats. Do not treat them with cruelty, just defeat them with strength. Even at the moment of triumph, observe your reactions and feed your angel and not the demon inside you. If you jump up with happiness, even mentally, for your actions of force against your enemy, you are doing the wrong thing, given that you are feeding your own demon with passion, which it is its food and so we are making it grow stronger.

Essentially we are living with our enemy inside ourselves. It is very simple to recognize what is our condition, but because our enemy is so astute, it disguises hate subtly into different forms like resentment, dissolution, indignity, disappointment and frustration. These are the catalysts that open the doors of our soul to embrace hate, rancor, ire, fury and anger which are the feelings of evil, conducting us to experience fear, anxiety, depression, stress, emotional trauma, despair and unhappiness which in turn make us suggestible to be controlled by the hypnosis in the hands of the oppressor.

The process of thinking performed by the mind is energized by the fuel contained in the soul. If the soul is mainly evil, your thoughts will be bad and your actions will follow the leader, they will also be bad, designed to cause pain and disgrace to the existence of others. Pain, sadness, disgrace, hate produce negative vibrations in the victim's soul, this in turn produces the food from which the resident Demon in our soul needs to remain alive and to grow.

When we do not know how these energies operate, we refuge in escapism or entertainment of any kind to get rid of the stress that these pressures exert over us. We need to keep our mind occupied by watching more sports, working harder, watching more movies, more pornography, eating more sophisticated food, drinking more alcohol, inventing new gender disorientation, more collections of toys, more compulsive purchasing, more new drugs, etc.

The enemy is Satan who uses different artifices and stratagems to entice his victims. He uses the image of the Antichrist, as if it were the a clown, conducting the orchestration from afar, at remote control since it has demons inside us—if we used computer terminology, it would be as having "cookies" in our system ready to turn into viruses at any moment—with the objective to manipulate our minds for his benefit, to produce his energy-food for his nurturing.

Money is the medium to obtain power which is the main tool to produce the emotional food for Satan to be nurtured. He uses his *invisible hands* to move his puppets according to his needs. His demons, angels of the darkness, form legions that infiltrate the souls of politicians, business people, clergyman of any religion or cult, any person holding at least a little bit of power, and the rest of the population that by dealing with any of the previous power holders, engage their souls as an extension of their master playing their mind roles as if they were the empowered puppets themselves, turning everyone into bio-cells of the anti-Christ. Reason to conclude that after using a little bit of our uncommon common-sense, that all of us use to be responsible for our own destiny; the destiny of our own country and the destiny of the planet earth. The ocean waters are absorbing the vibrations of the human kind and changing its structure constantly to more negativism, causing more water-related disasters in the future. Remember that water retains the information we are emitting, so whatever the humans have in their soul as a group, will have direct influence on water being 1/3 of the positive energy the proportion to keep the earth safe, without too much natural accidents affecting the human population. Leaving the negative side with the other 2/3 to the counterpart which by mere coincidence produces a decimal of 0.666, the number recognized as Satanic. It seems as if earth needs to keep a balance between negative and positive in the fulcrum of energies, a point of resonance. If this balance is interrupted, the negative invisible recipient does not get its doses of negative food. As we saw before, Satan receives energy from the suffering and disgrace of humans; if this suffering overpasses the point of resonance, the negative effect would generate the waters, which record human's energies within itself, uncontrollable, causing disasters on earth, destroying the human element, eliminating the source of negative energy needed by the negative recipient before mentioned, as if water defended itself. The same results happen with fire and wind. And obviously if the point of resonance does not occur for falling short of negative stimuli, the mayhem necessary is not produced either.

If you do not believe this, just look how the entertainers are so important before our eyes, they are into sports, movies and music. We have made them our escape route; we put them on pedestals; we make them our heroes; we make them our moral images to emulate. They keep us away from ourselves, creating those good imaginary lives that we dreamed about living ourselves, in other words, we keep our mental sanity by watching them act their roles as if they were ourselves. On the other side, observe our politicians, making illogical moves designed to disrupt the integrity of their own country, making people angry and frustrated, pushing us to the entertainers to keep us cool. We need to breake this line of thinking. Stop the eternal suffering, the usurpation, the insult, the indignity. Let us pray for those who want us to fall in disgrace and ***"forgive them, for they do not know what they are doing"*** as Jesus Christ said when he was crucified with two criminals in the Golgotha that gloomy and catastrophic afternoon. Let us change our destiny by conquering ourselves to reach the reward of happiness in our lives once and for all. But let us start now.

REFERENCES

SOME CONSULTED BOOKS

Psychosomatic	by Howard Lewis
The Merck Manual 1997	by Merck R. Labs
The Taber Medical Dictionary	by F. A. Davis
The Brain that Changes Itself	by Norman Doidge
Inside the Brain	by Ronald Kotulak
The Great Pyramid	by Rodolfo Benavides
Your Miracle Brain	by Jean Carper
Mind Performance Hacks	by Ron Hale-Evans
Mind Games	by Michael Powell
The 7 Habits of Highly Effective People	by Stephen R. Covey
Atlas of Anatomy 2002	by TAJ Books LTD 2002
The Father of Spin (E. Bernay)	by Larry Tye
Strange Stories, Amazing Facts 1978	by The Reader's Digest
The Schwarzbein Principle	by D. Schwarzbein
The Teachings of Don Juan	by Carlos Castaneda
Jesus, the Son of Man	by Gibran Jahlil Gibran
First and Last Freedom	by J. Krishnamurti
Foot notes	by Wikipedia

Printed in the United States
By Bookmasters